Praise for *Conflict in Relationships*

er handling of conflict in relationships is a critical life
career skill, yet far too few know how to do it well. Read
book and you'll learn how.. and... improve your life
career immeasurably in the process!"

t Cleland
der and President of Precursor

oundbreaking! A major work! This is the only book
the common reader... As a former executive of sixteen
rs, I feel that Conflict is also an excellent management
del... Bravo, bravo to the authors! This will be a classic."

E. Kent
ner CFO, US Department of State

today's market environment, rarely does a book come
ng that offers more than partial or superficial answers to
ic, real-life questions. Yet *Conflict in Relationships* is just
h a book – easily readable but not simplistic; profound
practical."

J Taylor
( ), Open Doors International

must-read for everyone, and a great teaching aid to
ble people locked in destructive conflict to find hope."

J e Davidge
Lic sed Marriage, Family and Child Therapist, Los Angeles, California

"Conflict is a normal part of life. It is as guaranteed as death and taxes, yet inside it lies an opportunity for more education than most classrooms can offer."

Jennifer Leech
Lawyer, Pastoral Care Minister at Port City Community Church.org

"Counsellors, Life Skills trainers and, most importantly, the individuals and couples they work with, can all benefit from reading this book."

Penny Flint
RELATE counsellor and writer

"... full of examples of real people I can relate to. And best of all, the concept of IC is challenging but practical and achievable."

Carol Blane
COSCA accredited counsellor, Deputy Manager Crossreach Counselling, Lothians, Scotland

A Lion Book
an imprint of
Lion Hudson plc
Wilkinson House, Jordan Hill Road,
Oxford OX2 8DR, England
www.lionhudson.com

ISBN 978 0 7459 5362 5

Distributed by:
UK: Marston Book Services, PO Box 269, Abingdon, Oxon, OX14 4YN
USA: Trafalgar Square Publishing, 814 N. Franklin Street, Chicago, IL 60610
USA Christian Market: Kregel Publications, PO Box 2607, Grand Rapids,
MI 49501

First edition 2010

10 9 8 7 6 5 4 3 2 1 0

Acknowledgments
pp. 111–14: Items taken from the Francis Psychological Type Scales, ©Leslie
J. Francis, 2005. The instrument was first published in Leslie J Francis (2005,
Faith and Psychology: Personality, Religion and the Individual. London:
Darton, Longman and Todd.
pp. 119–130: "Style Matters: The Kraybill Conflict Style Inventory", is
copyrighted material included under special license of the publisher,
Riverhouse ePress, and can be reproduced only by permission of the publisher.
A 14-page *Trainers Guide* with detailed instructions for guiding a group through
an interactive learning experience about conflict styles can be downloaded at
no cost from its publisher, Riverhouse ePress. A 24-page version with expanded
interpretation and strategic guidance is available for $4.95 in a downloadable
PDF file, and rights to reproduce it for group use can be purchased for $2.95.
Go to www.RiverhouseEpress.com or email: Center@RiverhouseEpress.com.
pp. 143–47: Material on conflict levels taken from *Moving Your Church through
Conflict* by Speed B. Leas with permission from the Alban Institute. Copyright
© 2006 by The Alban Institute, Inc. Herndon, VA. All rights reserved.

This book has been printed on paper and board independently certified
as having been produced from sustainable forests.
A catalogue record for this book is available
from the British Library

Typeset in 10.5/14 Baskerville BT
Printed and bound in Great Britain by J F Print Ltd., Sparkford, Somerset

SARA SAVAGE & EOLENE BOYD-MACMILLAN

Conflict
in Relationships

UNDERSTAND IT
OVERCOME IT

LION

Sara dedicates this book to Mark, Julie, and Liz
Eolene dedicates this book to Ron, Becky, and Jill

Contents

PART ONE

Conflict – it's about the two of you

Stella and Rachel used to be really good friends. Family histories, date debriefs, "Do I look OK in this?" were all part of the package. They had their own lingo and inside jokes. But since that one disagreement, things changed. They'd have long conversations trying to work it out but would end up shouting or hanging up.

For Stella and Rachel, things might get a lot worse or a lot better. The road to transforming conflict brings us to new places. It brings us to a whole new outlook on ourselves, our loved ones, our lives, our worlds. It involves how we see ourselves and other people, what we see and don't see, how we react to those with whom we strongly disagree, and how we feel our way through the conflict into a new place.

We have written this book because recent research has revealed that a human skill involving Integrative Complexity, or IC for short, is a crucial ingredient for conflict transformation. Developed by psychologist Peter Suedfeld[1] and his colleagues as a method for coding the complexity of thought, IC encompasses the latest understandings of whole-person conflict resolution and decision-making. There are seven levels of IC and everyone has a general baseline IC level. Conflict transformation involves ascending these levels after our IC has plummeted in response to the stress of conflict. Ultimately, we learn to work across the various levels of IC, depending on the relationship and context.

We have pioneered putting the steps of IC into action and have developed a new way of training people to transform even the most difficult of conflicts. At the invitation of the Foundation for Church Leadership (FCL), funded by the Henry Smith Charities, we conducted a major research project on conflict amongst senior church leaders who strongly oppose one another on key issues.[2] Working with bishops and equivalents across six denominations throughout the United Kingdom, we developed the only holistic training method for increasing capacities for conflict transformation using IC. The training successfully deals with our natural defensive reactions when we are in the heat of conflict. It involves not just how we think and feel but how our bodies respond and how we understand our world, our deepest values, and our identities. We know of no other approach as holistic.

Unprompted, the senior church leaders started to apply our approach to all of their close relationships – with family members, and friends, as well as with colleagues. It worked. We couldn't find a single relationship context where our approach didn't bring transformation. So Eolene taught it in care skills courses for faith communities and in courses for mental health practitioners (at the University of Edinburgh and on COSCA[3]-accredited counselling training courses). As one student said, "This is life-changing... these are core skills for human existence!" We agree. So Sara applied the principles to relational conflicts arising from fundamentalisms and religious extremism. If our approach brings transformation to these tense relationships, then it can work anywhere! Our colleague José Liht works with Sara in this area and contributed numerous insights, especially in Chapter 7.

We are not alone in our enthusiasm for the transforming potential of conflict. Business consultants,[4] counselling therapists, experts on creativity, scientific researchers,[5] and educational specialists[6] recognize conflict as inherent to innovation and success. Strategies ranging from "polarity management"[7] to "integrative thinking" and using your "opposable mind"[8] also recommend conflict as a ladder that can take our business, science, artistic creations, or thinking in any field to a higher level. Spiritual wisdom across the major religious traditions also treats conflict as an opportunity to discern God's invitation.[9] Creativity and growth in all areas of life come about not despite but because of multilevelled conflicts.

Many books claim to deliver a "conflict-free life".[10] We don't. Defining the successful life as conflict-free could be psychologically damaging. Conflict cannot be avoided; it is part of the DNA for human learning. To aim for conflict-free is to be set up to fail. The way our brains and bodies work, the way we operate as social beings, the way we live, love, and work, all involve conflict. Opposition. Struggle. Tension. Disagreement. To be part of this world is to engage with conflict and its potential for transformation.

The tools and skills taught in this book are akin to spiritual practices. They take us on a journey inward and outward, to discover how we function and how we can grow to become an agent of transformation in our relationships, organizations, and communities. Throughout this book we talk about "loved ones". We use this phrase in its broadest sense, to refer to those for whom we have grudging goodwill because they're human beings, as well as to those with whom we've made our deepest, most intimate commitments. Love is a part of every relationship. If we're in conflict with someone, on some level we care about them. People we don't care about at all don't elicit enough reaction from us to lead to conflict. We just move on.

The conflict scenarios we give throughout the book represent a range of relationships: friends, family, spouses, partners, colleagues, bosses, and children. The scenarios are from real-life situations but have been modified to preserve confidentiality.

Part 1 (Chapters 1–5) provides the vital understanding and steps that lead to conflict transformation within our relationships: friends, family, spouses, partners, colleagues, fellow volunteers. With learning exercises and illustrations, the chapters reveal the physiological and social obstacles to conflict transformation, and offer a tried and tested way to engage with the dynamics of conflict, even with "difficult" people.

In Part 2 (Chapters 6–8), we move into the bigger picture. What is going on behind the scenes? Conflict is not just about the two people locking horns but includes the social groups they belong to, their world views, their families, cultures, and religious backgrounds. These chapters explore how to increase conflict transformation skills far and wide through how we parent, teach, work, lead, and deal with religious conflict. In an era of increasingly complex threats to human survival, this is an urgent task.

We are deeply grateful to Revd Dr Fraser Watts, the director of our research team, the Psychology and Religion Research Group at the University of Cambridge, for enabling us to develop our approach to conflict transformation and to write this book. His unfailing kindness, good humour, calm in the midst of challenge, and belief in our work has supported us throughout. We are also grateful to our other colleagues who contributed their time and multiple talents to our research: José Liht, Liz Thompson, and Megan Hunter. We thank Malcolm Grundy and the FCL Trustees for commissioning the research and training. We thank Dave Richards, Jane and Duncan MacLaren, Seamus Prior, Andrea Wigglesworth, and Vicky McEvoy for their teaching invitations and openness to newly developed curriculum. Thanks also to Emma Greenfield, Bernadette Campbell, and Elizabeth White for bravely reading earlier drafts and offering valuable feedback. Finally, our thanks go to Kate Kirkpatrick at Lion Hudson for catching the vision of this book and for her enthusiasm and assistance during the writing.

CHAPTER 1

Relationship Conflict Boot Camp

Conflict happens – all the time. It's part of life. It's in the news, in relationships, inside us. Right now you might be in an inner conflict: should you keep reading or put this book down?

You might be in conflict with another person. A good friend, colleague, family member, or fellow volunteer. Your boss. Your closest loved one.

We enter into relationships with the hope of harmony and joy. Then we have our first fight. Suddenly our loved one has become our hated one. We react. A volcano erupts from within. It's all their fault. We overreact. We are in danger of destroying the very relationship upon which we depend.

Sometimes it's not that dramatic. But whether it's life-changing stuff or who does the dishes, this book offers a way through. It provides strategic relationship skills to transform conflict into a gift that transforms us. In the drama of relationship conflict, on stage are the brains, bodies, emotions, thoughts, values, and differing world views of each party. Oh – and the issue that sparked it – so often lost in the ensuing blaming and shaming. You may recognize something of yourself in the following conflict:

Jan had a plan – a *good* one about how to divide the holiday period equally between both their families. But, no, her loved one disagrees. Refuses to see it. She is left holding the shreds of her good idea. The metallic taste of sadness comes first. Tightness grips around her throat. Is this fear? She holds in her breath while her loved one shoots down her plans.

Jan thought she knew this person. But here is the reality. Her point of view is being trashed – on purpose, no matter how much this hurts her. This is not fair. This is unreasonable. It feels as if *she* is being trashed, along with her plan. Now Jan feels the rush of heat, her heart beating fearlessly, blood pumping like a crusader. She is catapulted on to a high horse of anger.

Jan's vision goes tight and focused. She sees things clearly now, in black and white. The background fades away. She sees that – really – her loved one is the aggressor here. Selfish and obtuse, as always. Positive memories of the relationship have vanished. She, the victim, must protect herself. A violent flood of words is forced from her mouth. She can't help it. She launches forth: "You always... You never... You are so..." She doesn't mean what she's saying, but it feels as if this is about life and death, right and wrong. She must stand her ground.

Meanwhile, Jan's loved one sees Jan as the attacker, as unreasonable. It is *Jan's* words that flay, destroy, and humiliate. Her loved one will not stand for this. Doors slam. Poisonous thoughts remain.

It's a battle for survival
In conflict, only one person can be right; only one person can

survive. That may sound extreme, but that is how our brains respond, even when conflict is about the small stuff. Simply the anticipation of conflict is enough to shift the brain into survival mode.

Does this mean Jan's relationship is over? Possibly. This argument may be one tiff in a long line of unresolved tiffs. Perhaps she is secretly looking for a way to end the relationship. Perhaps changing partners is easier than trying to change herself and the way she handles relationships.

Perhaps Jan really wants to make the relationship work but she's scared that it's too late. Here is the good news: conflict can be a turning point for the relationship and the people involved. We can figure out how to make our relationships work. Conflict can be a gift, in disguise.

It's the most important moment in the life of the relationship so far
This critical moment, if grasped, can form the future template for an honest, liberating relationship. The goal is not to make all conflict go away but to make conflict transformative. If we are afraid of conflict and think it is inherently "bad", then we will always try to avoid it. We'll never discover that most often the best outcome means facing into conflict.

Along with educational specialists, experts on creativity, leadership gurus, and scientific researchers, we recognize conflict as a vital part of the learning process. Discoveries and insights come about not despite but because of conflicts.[1] Conflict is a neutral dynamic that can be harnessed for good or ill. The practice of conflict transformation not only uncovers new insight on multiple levels, it creates a new framework to understand ourselves and our relationships. Feelings and relationships are transformed.

As we, the authors, have taught conflict transformation

to bishops, CEOs, writers, young people of different faiths, scientists, musicians, and counsellors in training, we have found that most people *hope* that conflict can be a positive force.[2] They just didn't yet have the understanding and skills to make that hope a reality. But with training, this changes.

Welcome to Boot Camp: A place of self-discovery

Over the next few chapters, we get to know ourselves better through Conflict Boot Camp. Conflict transformation is hard work. Nothing less than a serious boot camp for our minds, bodies, feelings, spirits, and behaviours will enable us to manage conflict in important relationships. In boot camp, we will discover a new framework for seeing ourselves and the other person in the midst of a raging conflict. We can use this framework on any relationship: with partners, spouses, close friends, family, children, in-laws, colleagues, bosses, subordinates, religious fellow-believers, and those people with whom we are locked in the closest kind of entanglement – our enemies.

Introducing IC (Integrative Complexity) = "I see"

The framework is simple. It involves *seeing* other points of view, even those with which we violently disagree, in all their complexity. In any conflict, there are at least two viewpoints: ours and the other's. The catch is listening to and respecting these clashing points of view. That is the hard part. We find it intensely threatening and annoying that other people see things differently from us.

Delving beyond the concrete specifics of clashing points of view, we discover deeply held values. He may value togetherness; she values independence. He may desire fairness; she desires compassion. They may want justice; we want liberty. If we can perceive some validity in the different values, we have begun the process of conflict transformation. Psychologist Peter Suedfeld[3] describes the structure of this kind of thinking in terms of its Integrative Complexity, or IC for short. IC sounds like "I see", which is convenient because IC is all about "seeing" deeply and accurately our own viewpoint and its underlying values, while at the same time perceiving deeply and accurately another's viewpoint and values.

Two steps: Branching out and weaving together
IC involves two steps. We call the first step of IC "branching out", or "branching" for short.[4]

The first moment of conflict feels like a breakdown within ourselves, with our loved one, and in our immediate world. This breakdown feels chaotic, and our knee-jerk reaction is to close down our thinking. I am right; they are wrong. What we need to do is the opposite. The feeling of breakdown can also motivate us to open up, look around, and branch out in our thinking.

1) *Branching out*
Imagine sitting on a branch in the thick of the prickly tree of conflict. We view the conflict from our defended position. We find it hard to see the other branches, other points of view, because we're so preoccupied with the leaves, twigs, and thorns on our

own branch. To get out of our stuck, defended, closed-down position, we need to look beyond to see the other branches, to see the whole tree.

Until we branch out, we see things in black and white: my branch, my position (the right one), and their branch, their position (the wrong one). Branching is the process of seeing that there is more than one way to look at what is going on. We begin to see that there is some validity in their point of view. We sort of "get" the other viewpoint, what they're aiming for. We have glimpsed something of what they value, what is deeply important to them, even though we still disagree with what they are saying.

We call the second step of IC "weaving together", or "weaving"[5] for short.

2) Weaving together

We gather together the different branches, the different points of view and values. We seek to weave those branches together in a way that makes sense of the situation, a way that has greater coherence than the simple sum of the parts. We may have to climb high up the tree to view the conflict from a whole new angle, in order to get a wider view that encompasses the clashing viewpoints. We don't just heap all the viewpoints together into a stack of disconnected branches.

As we begin to see all the different viewpoints from this higher vantage point, we try out different ways of weaving them together. We aim for a solution that meets the core values of all parties. We keep our own stance, retaining our own values. Weaving is not about settling for a muddy compromise or giving up what is vital to us. This is the creative part and involves some trial and error to respect the integrity of both parties. Weaving is the process of integrating those parts of our own and opposing viewpoints to achieve win–win solutions.

As a result of all our effort, expanded perception, and thinking, we come to a deeper understanding of our conflict partner and ourselves. Trust begins to be restored. Our relationship begins to be transformed. We emerge strengthened. Our enemy is our friend again, and life looks more hopeful. (We will revisit the branching and weaving in Chapters 2, 3, and 4.)

The egocentric default position of humanity

It sounds good, but none of this is easy. Initially, many of us react badly to conflict. Surely our perspective is the correct one. Why else would we see it that way? We are not crazy. Others may be, but certainly we can see what is going on.

This egocentric position is the normal, default position of humanity. Only with practice do we discover that we are not the centre of the universe. Reality is so rich and complex that it is normal for people to view things from very different perspectives. In fact, other people may discover aspects of the rich, mysterious, human reality that *we* cannot see. It takes humility to acknowledge that our viewpoint might be only partial.

But this is hard for us because when the one we love turns into the one we hate, our thinking closes down. We are threatened, and our thinking becomes less complex, more black and white. When times are good, we may have a generally complex way of thinking and seeing the world, but under threat we close down. We are no longer open to different ways of seeing.

This is borne out in decades of research on political proceedings, speeches, and negotiations.[6] The studies reveal a strong relationship between IC and violent conflict. When IC plummets from its normal baseline, violent confrontation is nigh, between groups, between individuals. To bring about a peaceful resolution to a conflict, both hostile parties need to raise their IC. But conflict makes us want to freeze, flee, or turn around and fight back.[7] No time for saying thoughtfully, "I see..." (IC); we have a visceral reaction telling us that on some level, however seemingly trivial, this conflict is about our survival.

Boot Camp preview, chapter by chapter

Our reaction to conflict begins in our brain. When threatened or under stress, our brain, especially the older, deeper part of the brain, switches gear and then drives the conflict process deeper. Many studies with brain scans document that even during trivial conflict our brain shifts into a survival gear. This is the first obstacle we need to tackle in Boot Camp. We introduce brain gear-shifting in **Chapter 2** (My brain made me do it). This chapter examines what is going on in our brains, why we find ourselves caught up in the heat of the moment, and how we can slow down the brain engine, so that we are able to perceive ourselves and others in the conflict more clearly. With this clearer perception can come more choice: how do I really want to behave in this situation? What is the bigger picture for this relationship? What do I want out of it? Reflecting on these questions will motivate us for the hard work of conflict transformation.

Chapter 3 (My group made me do it) opens up the social nature of human life. We enter into conflict not just as isolated individuals but as members of groups. (Our group is the best, of course.) We perceive others with whom we are in conflict as representatives of their groups (which are not as good as our own). Thus, any conflict between two individuals is also a conflict between, for example, family, ethnicity, or religious groups. Our loyalties to other people bias how we perceive conflict. If we can perceive our own biases, then we are on the road to conflict transformation.

Chapter 4 (Peacemaking armoury: Tools, strategies, skills) provides what we need to transform conflict. It takes hard work, but, with IC, we begin to see ourselves and our relationships in a new way. We offer an array of integrated life skills to use in different contexts and relationships. Core skills include active listening skills, self-discovery quizzes, a grid for appraising any conflict level, and a breakdown of the two-step IC framework just described. There will be memory aids, practice exercises, and examples for each item in the armoury so that we emerge from this phase of Boot Camp saying, "Bring it on: I can transform conflict!"

Chapter 5 (You made me do it) applies the two-step lens of IC to other people. Our first response is to blame others for the conflict we are in. The IC way of seeing can help us to engage even with very difficult people, people who themselves are unable, for whatever reason, to deal with clashing perspectives. We may value these people and want to approach conflict with them in a way that prevents harm and promotes growth. Yet we cannot change other people, so we need to adapt how we engage with "difficult people" during conflict so that we can still experience transformation.

Chapter 6 (My parents made me do it) starts to draw

the big map. Historically, we see human society as leading towards greater complexity, greater diversity. We now live in an era that requires ever greater abilities to work with many clashing points of view. This is the nature of our globalized, multicultural world. We look at how parenting styles may have affected us, and how they can help or hinder young people in our care to have their own perspective, have their own voice, and to give that same consideration to others. We briefly look at the school and work environments for their potential to cultivate leadership skills that include IC management. We *can* equip the next generation to transform conflict.

Chapter 7 (My religion made me do it) addresses the reality that religion can be the greatest stumbling block to conflict resolution. We cannot ignore this in an age of religious violence and terrorism. Yet we become part of the problem when we take a low-IC stance toward religion. The vast majority of the world's population is religious, and we can learn to resolve conflict with religious people. Religious faith has a dual dynamic. It can both nourish conflict transformation, and it can thrust us back into low IC when under threat. Maximizing the liberating and peace-making potential of faith requires "I see" (IC) in all its richness.

Chapter 8 (A guide to being an agent for peace: I can do it) brings Relationship Conflict Boot Camp to a conclusion with a summary map for transforming conflict. We can all be peacemakers in the midst of conflict with loved ones, friends, and colleagues.

Boot Camp induction

We are here

X Conflict = Disappointment
"Help! Get me out of here!"

Everyone entering Relationship Conflict Boot Camp has a common starting point: disappointment. Something in one or more relationships has gone wrong. We are embroiled in conflict. Most of us had high hopes for our close relationships, personal and professional. We hoped for true love, faithful partnerships, and blissful lives with enriching, stimulating friends and professional colleagues, but it's all been so much more difficult than we imagined.

Many people feel this. Expectations for relationships are higher. Yet we live in an era when close relationships easily unravel. Divorce. Serial monogamy. Living together; moving out. Friendships that go bust. Working relationships that break down. Recombined families. Starting over again. The costs of broken relationships are huge. Despite all the upheaval and heartache, we all desire close relationships more than ever. Bookstores are awash with self-help for relationships, and our own shelves may be lined with some of those books. Relationship repair is a growth industry. We are searching for the key to repair relationships.

Do we need to ditch our relationship books to try IC? No. The IC approach complements and deepens the relationship advice that is out there. This advice can be located within three main approaches to understanding the push and pull factors in relationship conflict: the biological, social, and unconscious approaches.

Three major approaches to understanding relationships

Approach 1: Our bodies' marching orders

We are driven into the arms of those we love. No one doubts the power of sex. Biological cues generate desires for non-demanding closeness, cuddling, and foreplay. When the bonding hormone oxytocin floods our bloodstream, we feel safe and full of bliss. We are able to trust and grow close. In contrast, the hormones released by orgasm play a different role. After a few hours, those hormones encourage distance between the couple who soon begin to get on each other's nerves once the post-coital glow has worn off.[8] Nature's aim has been achieved, at least temporarily. So move on. Thus biology entices us together and can push us apart.

When we find ourselves bickering, in conflict about the (in)frequency of lovemaking or its perfunctory nature, what should we do? Freeze, flee, or fight? What's the advice on offer? The advice is to slow down and reflect on the last time you and your loved one engaged in low-key, non-demanding expressions of affection. Intercourse usually stirs up anxiety about performance. An impromptu back rub, arm-in-arm stroll, or seated hand-holding without moving to intercourse bonds us together with the glue of oxytocin. The sources of irritation will either disappear or become much less potent. This kind of bodily strategy is very important for some conflict situations, as our physical, hormone-laden bodies do play a role in conflict of any kind. In Chapter 2, we aim to transform the stress reaction of our bodies when in conflict;

we do not need to be controlled by the initial reactions of our brain and body.

Approach 2: Social marching orders

The next major approach to what makes or breaks relationships is social. All the world's a stage and never more so than in conflict. This approach coincides with the next phase of Boot Camp (Chapter 3): raising the curtain on the social drama of conflict.

Our life experience teaches us our social worth; we know what level we are pegged at, and, in relationships, we trade at that level. This applies in friendship and professional relationships as much as in marriage. Conflict-free relationships are about getting a fair exchange, something for something.[9] In this exchange, we might try to get from our partner something we feel we lack in ourselves. We love in them what we lack in ourselves. It can work well if we connect with someone who counterbalances our dominant personality traits. He's the life of the party; she's shy and reserved. Conflict arises when unfairness (again, real and perceived) occurs. Topics of marital conflict are usually about sex, money, children, and in-laws: who is getting more, who is getting less. Many conflict strategies for regulating "fairness" seek to exchange something for something. "You pick up your socks from the floor and I'll bake you your favourite cake." To reduce conflict, make fair exchanges.

Times of change can tip the balance of fair exchange. Marriages often break up in the first year ("Oops, we made a mistake") and after the first child ("Whoa – I can't take all these changes and demands"), or when people come from very different backgrounds, exacerbated by family disapproval.

Overall, the approaches that focus on biological and

social forces seem to notice how like mixes with like, or that at least the similarities are strongly perceived early on, even if differences are recognized further down the road. Conflict is minimized when a level of perceived fairness is maintained, and this can be easier when people are perceived as being not too different. Similar views, goals, and values all set the stage for a level of harmony. The attention given to famous couples with known opposing viewpoints underscores their unusualness. In the US, the marriage of Maria Shriver, a member of the powerful Democratic Kennedy clan, and Arnold Schwarzenegger, a Republican, generated more than a few column inches of press commentary. How could they marry when Republicans and Democrats are political enemies? Did they betray their ideals and beliefs for the sake of blind love? No one couple's experiences can serve as a template for others, and only Maria and Arnold really know how well or not they have managed to work out their differences. What we do know is that difference can be a great driver toward relational creativity, development, and growth, especially when the framework of "I see" (IC) is brought into play.

Another well-known strategy involves developing strong friendships outside of the marriage or close relationship. Some couples need to learn not to expect a partner to meet all of their relationship needs. No one person can be everything we need.

Yet another strategy involves accepting, letting go, and moving on. "Even when I bake your favourite cake, you still don't pick up your socks, so I am going to accept your messiness, let go of my frustration, and accept you as you are." Life is too short. The world will not collapse from dirty socks strewn across the floor. Some hassles are not worth hassling about. Again, this way of avoiding small conflicts works well in some situations. These fairness approaches to relationship conflict can be effective. They promote fairness, but no one has to change deeply.

Despite the usefulness of these various strategies to resolve conflict, if overused, they can miss out. They stop short of taking people on an empowering journey to transform conflict and deepen love. Developing the ability to see (IC) self and others will help us to identify when these approaches are useful and when we need to press beyond them toward transformation.

Approach 3: Unconscious drivers toward wholeness

The third main way of understanding what makes and breaks relationship has to do with our pasts. People often resist digging around in the past. But the past is not dead. The past is not even past. We see this through the repeating patterns in our lives. We keep starting out with high hopes for our close relationships, but then the same old pattern keeps repeating.

When we think we've found our soulmate, our bodies sing with delight, and we see ourselves gliding effortlessly towards a rosy future. What we don't realize is that our brand new relationship is a relatively blank canvas. Yes, a blank canvas because we hardly know the other person, really. On this blank canvas we unconsciously paint our deepest needs and pin our hopes that this person will meet them. We think our joy is from discovering this person's wonderful, unique, interesting, and amazing characteristics. But our excitement really comes from an unconscious expectation that they will be who we *want* them to be. They will complete the nurturing task that was left incomplete by our parents and carers.

Very few of us emerge into adulthood having had all our needs for security, love, affection, independence, and self-esteem met. Indeed, our needs are infinite and contradictory: we often want both belonging and independence. However wonderful our parents or carers have been, we come into adulthood unconsciously seeking to complete that unfinished project, getting our infinite and contradictory needs met. Leading marital therapist Harville Hendrix[10] says we are primed to find the person that best matches our composite image (or Imago) of our parents' good and bad qualities. When we've found a target, we lock on and move in. We select our mate to replay our early dramas, both the good and the bad. It's unfinished business, and we want a triumphant ending to our play.

The first fight is a shock. That other person is not meeting our needs. He or she is not making us whole. Whether the wholeness we are seeking is healing from our childhood wounds or completeness from reunion with parts of our personality suppressed through socialization, we urgently want to press our partner back into meeting our needs. Clicking with a friend or buzzing with a colleague means there has been some degree of match between some parts of our unconscious self and our new friend or associate. We're sensing the possibility of some wholeness. Our partner, friend, or colleague is sensing the same from us. Yet we are swimming at cross-purposes. Mix in the biological forces that draw and repel. Surround it all with social concerns about similarity, difference, and fair play. And the resulting toxicity can generate enough disappointment and frustration for a disaster site.

Conflict rips off the mask of the fun, cheerful "need-free" self we like to present in the early stages of our relationships.

Conflict also exposes that the real friend, partner, or colleague is quite different from what we had thought. The enchantment breaks both ways. We may begin to realize that we are, in fact, seeking our lost or disowned part of ourselves through the other person. We are faced with our own limits and the impossibility of someone else filling our emptiness. Conflict exposes the raw hurt of our unmet childhood needs. Our hope that our needs will be met is shaken. In fact, now that we can see the other person more accurately, we may come to realize that our friend, partner, or colleague is destined to wound us again. They have their own childhood wounds and dreams of healing. Not only can they not make us whole, they're not whole themselves. In all this disappointment, conflict is a moment of truth. It is the best learning experience on offer.

Why did we choose someone who replays the negative traits of our childhood carers as well? Harville Hendrix says that we are urged to complete unfinished business so that our personal childhood wounds can be healed. We choose someone with the good *and* the bad traits of our carers. Healing requires us to repeat the *negative* relationship patterns that began in childhood as well as the positive. There is no other way forward. We need all the conflict resolution skills we can get.

We tend to seek out people with the same wounding capacities of those who hurt us in our early lives, as well as the wonderful aspects. The daughter of an alcoholic father marries a heavy drinker who binge-drinks and passes out every weekend, but he is also a lot of fun and caring when sober. The young man with an emotionally distant mother forms a relationship with a career woman who works late and then ignores him, but she is also an insightful conversation partner and a great partner when she does focus on the relationship. There is a logic here, albeit contorted. Unrealistically, the daughter marries the heavy drinker hoping that she can transform him into the responsible non-alcoholic man her father was not. Unrealistically, the young man marries a busy, distracted woman who treats him coldly in the hope of transforming her into the attentive, relationally engaged woman his mother was not. In this way, we replay our childhood experiences of comfort and abandonment, of pleasure and pain, of joy and sorrow, in each close relationship.

This is not just self-sabotage. There is a hidden purpose: the healing and reworking of those damaging patterns. However, the healing does not happen magically. It will not happen if we unconsciously use other people to co-star in our internal dramas. (They never stick to the scripts we give them anyway. They have their own internal scripts, and are annoyed that we are not sticking to the lines they have written for us.) And so we fight with the ones we love, until we bring all these patterns into conscious awareness. The biological marching orders that draw us both together and apart, the social marching orders that look for fair exchange on all levels, and the unconscious drivers that propel us to seek our lost half and heal our childhood wounds, all coalesce to spark the conflicts that can destroy or transform the relationship. But wait, there's more.

Families of choice
It is not just our loved ones whom we expect to meet our needs. Through our marriages, close friendships, and organizational commitments, we want our "happy family" fantasy fulfilled. When we fall in love, we are looking for more than just our ideal partner. We are looking for our marriage

to create a whole womb-like self-sustaining community. We're looking for utopia. We marry each other's families; we think they will be better than our own! Surely my faith community or my best friend's family will be there for me in the way that my own never was. Surely the office parties and team-building trips will foster real loyalty and kindness toward one another.

Reality crashes in. Sometimes it is even better than we'd hoped. This is something to celebrate. But often we are disappointed with the community or organization, as well as with the social dynamics among our fellow members or colleagues. We are disappointed with the family system, as well as with the relationship. We are disappointed with the other person and with ourselves.

Strategies for wholeness

In a committed relationship, a track record of mutual harm may require skilled intervention. Disappointed hopes are often played out like a verbal tennis game: "You always…"; "No, you always…" Hurtful behaviours and demeaning dialogue may have to be tackled. These two-person dramas must be made conscious, and for this, intentional work is needed. This may be in the form of therapy with a marriage or relationship counsellor. We may need to decide to close our exits, which are used to avoid the deep work of intimacy.[11] And underlying these strategies to do with healing our past is the secret weapon of IC.

The secret weapon: IC ("I see")

The IC framework encompasses all three of the major approaches to understanding relationships (biological, social, and unconscious). We don't need to throw away our relationship self-help library. As an overarching framework, IC can help us negotiate biological and sexual forces that draw us toward someone and then drive us apart; it can help us negotiate social concerns about similarity, difference, and fair play; and it can help with the deeper unconscious desires for wholeness that blind us to ourselves and the other person. We can use the IC framework in this book on its own or in conjunction with other self-help books. The IC framework as part of the full armoury of conflict transformation will complement individual or couple counselling or any other supportive relationship (for example, spiritual direction, mentoring, coaching, group therapy) helping us through relational conflict. IC means we see ourselves and the other person more clearly.

I exist!

We might be tempted to interpret the language of owning our viewpoint as the language of entitlement: "My rights, my voice, this show is all about me!" Rather, we are encouraging something more foundational, to do with the core of our being. When we own our own viewpoint in a conflict, we are saying, "My experience is valid. This is how I feel. This is how I see things. It is valid to communicate my experience."

Beneath these statements is the fundamental idea: "I exist. I have the right to exist as me. I am an end in myself, not just a means for others to use for their own ends, their needs or wishes. All the different parts of me are real and have a right to be. I exist."

You exist

As social beings, we cannot exist in a vacuum. We have a viewpoint and other people have their viewpoints. If my perspective is valid, it immediately follows that the other person's perspective has some validity too. No matter how strongly we disagree with the other person's perspective, we can acknowledge that they have a right to their viewpoint. When we give another person permission to own their perspective, we are saying, "How you feel is valid. How you see things is valid. It is valid for you to communicate your experience."

Beneath these statements is the corresponding fundamental idea: "You exist. You have the right to exist as you. You are not just a projection of my needs and wishes. You are an end in yourself, not just a means for me (or others) to use for our own ends, needs, or wishes. All the different parts of you are real and have a right to be. You exist."

We disagree, but we can more than coexist…
we can love

With the framework of IC, we learn to see our own and the other person's perspectives. By doing so, we are recognizing the irreducibility of each person involved in the conflict. This recognition is not far from the command to love our neighbour as we love ourselves.

What is love? It can be helpful to recast this overused word in a new way. We like to think about love like this:

Love is the non-possessive, deep appreciation of, and delight in, the uniqueness of the other person, and their differences from us as well as their similarities.

A lot is packed into that sentence. If we are non-possessive, then we do not try to control the other person. We do not try to make them do what we want them to do or be who we want them to be. We will ask them to do something ("Please take out the recycling, the containers are overflowing") but ultimately it is their choice. We will ask them to be a certain way ("Be polite to my colleague, please; I know he's kind of obnoxious, but I have to get along with him") but again it is ultimately their choice. Another person is not a prize possession or trophy but someone who is choosing to be with us. If we really take that in, it can be breathtaking: "They are choosing to be with me. Wow. They see me as I am and still they are choosing to be with me."

This gratitude is not the same as a low self-esteem that is thankful for even a crumb of kindness. No, this amazement is a genuine appreciation that someone has recognized our worth and that we value them too.

This deep appreciation of the fully rounded nature of another person takes time and effort. We cast so many of our own projections on to the blank slate of the other person that we cannot even *see* let alone love them for who they really are. Not seeing, we are cut off from the other person.

The framework of IC creates a bit of distance, some separateness, in order to see ourselves and the other person more clearly. There will always be some distortion in either direction. Conflict will always be a gift, an opportunity for greater clarity and learning. Therefore, our own standpoint is vitally important. We have to see from somewhere, even if it is a tentative or transitional place. When we are glued to others, we can be blinded either by our own need, by our own shaping of the other person into what we want them to be, or by trying to meet their needs, thereby contorting ourselves. Either way, we lose ourselves and can't see them. We have to learn how to be connected *and* separate in order to become ourselves and to allow others to be themselves.

Paying attention to how we view ourselves and others is to take responsibility for the first step toward love. It is very hard to become more loving unless we focus on how we see and think. Our thinking is a very flexible part of ourselves. This flexibility is a defining feature of being human. No other living creature has the capacity to adapt to new conditions, test out new hunches, and develop new ways of thinking.

But my thinking can clash painfully with your thinking. And so we need to weave together an overarching, bigger viewpoint that does justice to these clashing viewpoints. This requires some critical distance from our viewpoint and from the view of the other person. We have to climb higher up the tree of conflict. The alternative is eventually meeting our loved one – spouse, neighbour, family member, colleague, friend – in court. The high cost of not resolving conflict in human and societal terms is huge. Don't go there. Read this book instead. The lives we save will not only be our own.

A spiritual journey

Weaving together the overarching view is a creative task, requiring insight. Finding the life-giving path that joins together the best of the clashing perspectives requires attitudes akin to traditional spiritual disciplines.

Humility is needed. Attention to detail is needed. Waiting, patience, and trust are needed. Hope and faith that the universe will be hospitable to different perspectives are needed. If we remain open, scanning for possible solutions, the weaving will reveal itself in due course. The best fit will emerge as we trial and error the specifics of both perspectives.

In the language of faith, it is as if the love of God, big enough to encompass both viewpoints, is embodied in the relationship. With this comes a realistic and, perhaps, humble solution that is ethical for both conflict partners. Reality has its limitations and not *everything* is possible. However small the initial insight may seem to be, the glimmer of a way forward that honours the clashing viewpoints is the beginning of something real, of infinite worth. Conflict is the birth pang that ushers us into *real* relationship.

So we conclude this Boot Camp induction with the cries not of war but of birth. And with the next chapter, we turn to the realities of our brains and bodies.

Note:

Domestic abuse and violence is prevalent both within and outside faith communities. Whatever your faith commitment (or none), if you are experiencing domestic violence, then you need to get out. International research has found roughly similar numbers of male and female violent abusers, although violence perpetrated by women is under-reported.[12] Unless the abusive partner is willing to look at themselves, accept responsibility, and get professional help concerning their need to dominate and control you (directly or through children), no amount of promised reform or pleas for forgiveness will lead to lasting change. This is a sad fact, yet borne out by every piece of research on the issue. Get help now, and, from a place of safety and security, hope and pray that the abusive person will seek help too.

CHAPTER 2

My brain made me do it

It is normal to feel conflict *in our bodies*. During conflict, our
 • pupils dilate
 • respiration increases
 • pulse races
 • blood stream is fuelled up with sugar for extra energy
 • muscles tense
 • stomach closes down – all energy is diverted away
from digestion and toward enabling us to move as fast as
possible.

This frenetic activity in our bodies prepares us to deal with danger.

Why do our bodies act like this? Our brains have sent out intense signals alerting our bodies that our very survival is at stake. We are ready to freeze, flee, or fight.[1] But we might not be in touch with all that's going on in our bodies. We just know that we feel really uncomfortable.

Flatmate J: You did it again, didn't you?!

Flatmate K: What?

J: Don't ask "What?" You know what. I've asked how many times.

K: Lighten up, will you? It doesn't matter.

J: It does matter. We have to pay our council tax on time. It goes on our credit record.

K: A couple of weeks is no big deal. We're fine.

J: How many times do I have to tell you? A couple of weeks is not fine. It goes on our – *MY* – credit record as being two weeks late. We've talked about this. You promised.

K: I don't need this. I'm out of here.

J: You bet you're out of here. Find a new place to live, bud. I'm not taking this any more.

During this conflicted encounter, K has displayed all three reactions: freeze ("What?"), fight ("Lighten up, will you? It doesn't matter... A couple of weeks is no big deal. We're fine"), and flee ("I'm out of here"). The tone may have been casual but the brain was fighting for survival.

Our brain has three layers. The inner layer is called the brain stem and it handles unconscious, automatic functions such as breathing and blood circulation. The middle layer is called the limbic system. Whenever we feel stressed or anxious, this middle layer of the brain goes into overdrive. The outer layer is called the neocortex, and it gears up whenever we are being analytical or rational.[2]

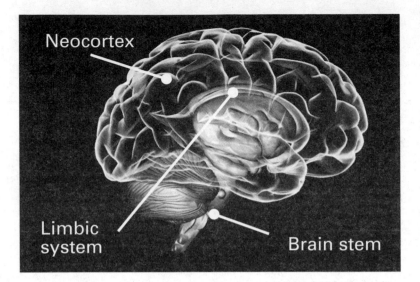

Our entire brain is active all the time, but brain scans show us which parts are extra-active during particular thoughts or feelings – such as the limbic system when we're feeling stressed and anxious. The workings of our brain present five challenges to seeing different points of view, which is the core of IC and conflict transformation.

1) The shouting match in my brain:
Limbic system v. neocortex

Conflict creates a contest in our brain between the limbic system and the neocortex, the middle and outer layers of the brain. During stress and anxiety, our brains have an inner conflict, and the middle layer wins hands down every time. The limbic system shouts louder than the neocortex.[3]

Stress or anxiety gets the limbic system shouting to the rest of the brain and body, "HIGH ALERT! DANGER!" The neocortex does a quick analysis of the situation, deciding in a heartbeat whether to freeze, flee, or fight.

> Colleague P: I told her. I told the boss. She wants to see you.

> Colleague R: What?

> P: She did not look happy.

> R: Who?

> P: Look, my husband has been laid off work. I can't lose this job. I had to make sure I didn't get blamed.

> R: What?

> P: You'll be fine. Just tell her what happened. Don't look at me like that! You look as if you're about to faint.

> R: I do?

Colleague R has frozen. He's not fighting. He's not fleeing. In his family and culture, you manage. Like the impala falling over and lying motionless so the cheetah stops, sniffs, and moves away, we hope our "enemy" – our colleague who has said something to our boss who now wants to see us – will think we're already dead and go away.[4] He hasn't expressed his feelings. What's the use? Later, he might explode in anger, or feel chest pains and hear the doctor reassure him that it's only a panic attack. He might stop getting out of bed in the morning. He wonders what's going on, not connecting his symptoms to the conversation with his colleague. He's forgotten about it. But his body hasn't. It's frozen in high alert and is breaking down under the pressure.

Any other input from the neocortex cannot be heard over the alarm of the limbic system. Messages from the neocortex – such as "It's OK. I'm not really in danger... I can walk away. I can listen. I can ask for time to respond... What they are saying does not define me or the situation... Breathe deeply. I will learn and grow through this experience" – do not penetrate the barrage of stress signals from the limbic system. Thoughts reminding us about the bigger picture – our personal power and freedom – don't get through the warning signals. It takes simple, targeted actions to slow down the limbic system so that the neocortex can present different points of view.

2) The filter in my brain: Binary thinking

Our brains "chunk" information. We filter into categories the enormous amounts of information constantly bombarding our five senses. Normally, this is a good thing. Without this filtering system we would be overwhelmed with information. We would struggle to communicate with other people without commonly recognized categories. Chunking information into categories helps us to connect with the world.[5] But, like any good thing, too much can be bad.

Under pressure from the limbic system, the neocortex simplifies by dividing everything into binary categories, into two groups. In reality, our conflict partner is both a foe *and* a friend. But our brains want us to choose one or the other. The theory is that our hunting and gathering ancestors would see an approaching speck on the horizon and have to make an instant decision about whether it was a friend or foe. Binary thinking helped our ancestors to survive. Today it can be lethal.

The BBC drama *Five Minutes of Heaven*[6] starred Liam Neeson and James Nesbitt. A Catholic raised in Northern Ireland, Neeson played a Protestant terrorist who had shot a Catholic in the Troubles. Neeson's character served twelve years in prison before being released for reconciliation work. He explains his journey:

For me to talk about the man I've become you need to know something about the man I was. I was fourteen when I joined the tartan gangs. Fifteen when I joined the UVF... the feeling was... We're all in this together and we have to do something... Once you have signed up to terror and joined the organization – The Group – your mind closes right down. It becomes only our story that matters. Not their story, the Catholics. It's only my people that are being killed... Catholics being killed? Doesn't enter your head. And so when... I wanted to kill a Catholic man, it wasn't a wrong thing for me to do. In my head it was the right thing to do, the proper, the just, the fair, the good thing to do. And so it was easy.

When I got home... I was so excited... everybody was going to stand up and applaud... me. I would have shot anyone for that... That's what it was like. I was only seventeen... You take sides with your friends as a boy, but we weren't just throwing stones, we were shooting guns.

... what society needs to do is to stop people getting to the point where they join the group. Because when you get to that point it's too late. No one's going to stop you. No one's going to change your mind. And once you're in, you will do anything. You will kill anyone on the other side because it's right to do it... And what he needs to hear are voices on his own side stopping him before he goes in... No one was telling me anything other than that killing is right. It was only in prison when I heard that other voice.

And the Muslims now, the kids now are like I was then. They need to hear those voices now, stopping them from thinking that killing is good... that is why I talk to anybody who will listen

to tell them to stop boys like me who think that to shoot an innocent
and a decent man in the head is a good thing.

Outside of sectarian violence, perhaps we don't see ourselves
this way, especially when it comes to arguing with those we
love. Sorry to be the bearers of uncomfortable news, but
this is exactly what we do. We all do. Even if we're not living
in the midst of any kind of overt violence, our brains divide
people into friends and foes. Everyone we're in conflict
with becomes a foe as far as our limbic system is concerned,
even those we love. That is part of the pain of conflict. My
loved one and I once had formed an "us" and now it feels
like my loved one has shattered that togetherness. There is
no sting like the anticipated, perceived, or actual sting from
someone we love.

Most of us avoid those with whom we disagree
vehemently. That's why it's so horrible when our flatmate,
closest colleague, or spouse morphs into one of "them".
Imagine being invited to have dinner with someone on
the other side of an issue we feel passionately about. We'd
find our diary was already full, or that it is vitally important
that we sort through our sock drawer. Merely anticipating
an encounter with someone activates our limbic system,
demanding a response from our neocortex: friend or
foe? It doesn't want a nuanced response. It wants a snap
judgment so it can tell the body whether to go into code
red or to step down. Whether with a stranger or a loved
one, an anticipated conflict means our limbic system thinks
our very survival is at stake. For the limbic system, it *is* life
or death.

She: I asked you to take out the recycling two days ago. It's overflowing now.

He: Oh, I forgot. I'll do it.

She: When?

He: I'll do it later.

She: But you'll forget again. Tell me when you'll do it.

He: Don't try to control me. I said I'd do it. I forgot, but now I remember.

She: I don't believe you. It's a mess. The papers are falling down all over everything. The bottles are lying around. It needs to be done now.

He: No. I'll do it later. Stop being a nag. It's not really that important. It will get done. I don't have to do something just when you say it.

She: You never do what you say you're going to do. I don't trust you. I can't take this.

He: If you're that bothered, do it yourself.

She: I always end up doing everything myself. (Tears flow.)

He: You cannot let something rest. I don't want this hassle. (Door slams.)

Recycling has taken on symbolic significance, for her of working together as a team, for him of unnecessary hassle. She feels abandoned and he feels smothered. It feels like life or death. Our desire to feel connected and separate is central to a lot of our relationship conflict, but our limbic system is separating everything into binary categories. We're either together or apart. We don't even hear our conflict partner; we hear the category we've put them into: they are wrong or bad because they disagree with us. The reality is that we will survive our feelings of abandonment or being smothered, and the related feelings of anger, frustration, fear, and grief. We can feel these feelings and learn to set or lower boundaries, to ask for and respond to requests for behaviour changes.[8] Life will go on and can even get a lot better. We can overcome this opposition to be a team again; we can become an "us" instead of a "me" versus "you".

3) The blinders in my brain:
Only one viewpoint correct (mine!)

In conflict, we literally do not see any point of view as valid as our own. As our limbic system sends out the alarm, our neocortex narrows our focus. *All* we really see is our own viewpoint. To the extent that we do see other viewpoints, we dismiss them as inadequate. This is how our brain works. We're not being stupid or showing a lack of education. Physiology is a great equalizer. Whatever our social status, IQ, or educational level, our brains in code red (anticipating or experiencing even a trivial conflict) will narrow our focus to ensure our survival.[9] Probably our ancestors had to be single-minded when trying to avoid prowling enemies or to track down food after three days of hunger. Any distraction could mean instant death by attack or starvation. Even minor conflicts could lessen the chances of survival. Those living today in war zones will be very conscious of what it's like to live with constant vigilance.

"Automatic" reactions: Slow to change, quick to return
A recent film can help us to imagine how our limbic system

operates. In the first film from the Bourne Trilogy, *The Bourne Identity*, Jason Bourne talks to his new friend about his amnesia.[10] Not only does he not know who he is, he doesn't know why he does what he does. He can't enter a room without instantly appraising every person's strength and hidden weapons, and identifying exit routes. This happens without intention. It feels automatic. His muscles twitch with readiness after every sudden noise or movement. Again, there is no conscious thought; it just happens. Even though we're not trained assassins, this is how our limbic system works. We're not conscious of anxiety about our survival; even if we are not aware that we feel tense.

A single-minded focus on survival during conflict constricts our thinking. It is almost impossible to see any point of view but our own. We don't have the mental energy that it might be a good thing to consider other viewpoints. They do not exist in any real sense until we humanize our conflict partners or they "humanize" us. In another trilogy, *The Lord of the Rings*,[11] a pathetic creature named Gollum displays a single-minded focus on his love, "my precious", an alluring gold ring that ensnares and destroys all who possess it or use it for power. Gollum loses the ring and now Frodo carries it, intending to destroy it. Tracking down Frodo with evil intent, Gollum experiences Frodo as compassionate and kind, and instead starts to trust Frodo. Gollum starts to see other points of view. Tragically, this ends when he feels betrayed by Frodo and his perspective constricts again. We, too, can be slow to trust, to see other points of view, and quick to return to a constricted outlook that dehumanizes those who think differently.

We may decry the dehumanization process that enabled people to commit the atrocities at Abu Ghraib or behead the CARE director, Margaret Hassan in Iraq in 2004, but we all have the capacity to dehumanize anyone who opposes us, and we do it all the time. We dehumanize in small ways. Snide remarks, the cold shoulder, condescending attitudes, and so on oppress and dehumanize others. We struggle to stop ourselves from behaving in this way. Why? We feel threatened. We anticipate or are in a conflict, and our limbic system is geared up. Is it inevitable that we are at the mercy of our brain structure and functioning ("My brain made me do it!")? No. We can strengthen the signals from our neocortex and use the vitality of our limbic system to transform the conflict with IC.

I'm not like that!

Most of us think that we're reasonable; we've considered the options, we're open-minded. We don't want to believe that we can be closed-minded. To experience the reality of how we see only our own viewpoint, look at the following:

Some people will see a vase and some will see two facing profiles. Most people flip back and forth between seeing the vase and the profiles.

In conflict, with effort, it is possible to see more than one viewpoint. Insights that can transform conflict involve figure–ground reversals. That is what is happening with the vase and profiles. First, we see the vase as the figure, and the profiles as the background. Then they reverse: the profiles become the figure and the vase the background. Then they reverse again and so on. At the highest level of IC (level 7), we integrate the figure and the ground into a larger prespective encompassing both. But we have to break out of our tunnel vision to learn to see the different perspectives, the figure *and* the ground, and accept their validity. It is very, very difficult to accept that, although we may disagree with them, different viewpoints have their own validity.

Think of a conflict you are in or experienced recently. Think of who was involved. Recall what was at stake. Reflect on your feelings.

What was your point of view?

Was there another point of view? If so, what was it? What did you think of it?

Trauma and tunnel vision

Our constricted focus, unable to see any viewpoint but our own, can be reinforced by a consequence of conflict: trauma. By trauma we mean a perceived or actual threat that overwhelms our ability to respond.[12] Feeling as if we have responded inadequately disempowers us profoundly. We berate ourselves for not standing up for ourselves, for being taken in by someone, for trusting or not trusting, and so on. Our body responds by conserving energy through a narrowed focus on survival. Connections with other people weaken as we turn in on ourselves. Unable to see any viewpoint but our own, the ongoing destructive conflict leads to more trauma. And the cycle goes on and on.

Trauma can result from something obvious such as an experience of war or rape, or something less obvious such as falling off a bicycle or being left alone as a child. Less obvious events are very individual, leaving one person traumatized and not another. A key factor seems to involve the compassion and support we feel from others at the time, the opportunity to talk about our feelings of stress and anxiety with people who express love and acceptance. The fallout from trauma can happen over time, a slow sapping of self-confidence, a slow withdrawal from certain activities or types of people, a constriction in our perspective. "In short, trauma is about a loss of connection – to ourselves, to our bodies, to our families, to others, and to the world around us."[13] The crucial factors are the perception of threat and the inability to do anything about it.

In trauma, our sense of self is "pierced" (the meaning of the Greek word from which "trauma" comes) and we lose our ability to navigate our world. Analytical reasoning becomes very difficult. Our sense of space and time becomes distorted; visual cues do not compute. We blank. Lose our train of thought. Forget where we are going. Wonder what life is about. Those working with traumatized people can experience what is called "vicarious trauma"; that is, they experience symptoms of trauma even though they have not lived through the traumatic experiences. Social workers, health-care workers, court system workers, home carers, foster carers, citizen's advice workers, therapeutic and counselling workers... vast numbers of people trying to help traumatized people become vicariously traumatized themselves. Trauma also affects family members who are worried about and compensating for their distressed family member. The statistics for over-eating, over-drinking, over-spending, and other forms of distraction and "self-medicating" indicate trauma on an almost unimaginable scale.

People who overcome trauma have an inner strength

called "resilience" that enables them to survive. They bounce back from the traumatic experience rather than become entrapped in it. Schools and counsellors now instruct people on nurturing their own resilience, helping trauma survivors to access their inner resources to move beyond the trauma. Yet focusing on resilience as the silver lining in trauma risks accepting the underlying individual, social, and structural causes, even normalizing them. The preventable causes of trauma, such as sexual abuse, violence, and destructive conflict, move out of the spotlight. Resilience can become a quick fix that fails to recognize the breadth and depth of harm that accompanies trauma, even when one appears to bounce back.[14]

Some argue that the rapid technological, social, and economic changes involving vast upheavals in a postmodern, globalized world have left whole cultures and societies traumatized.[15] Just as the rubble of war-torn cities reflects an explosion of human strife, perhaps the current environmental crisis is symptomatic of a human crisis, both showing symptoms of trauma.[16] Even without macro-level upheavals, however, we all enter the world through a traumatic process of near suffocation as we leave the womb. We come into life already fearing for our survival and struggling to orient ourselves. Stressed (although a newborn's brain is not fully developed, the limbic system will be sending out strong alert signals), we respond by moving into a symbiotic relationship with the "other" who feels closest and safest, our primary carer. We adapt to the needs and desires of our primary carers. When older, we might try to separate by adapting the opposite perspective. This isn't really *our* perspective; it's just a reactive anti-stance. Still, it represents a step forward.

Surprise: A step forward that looks like a step back
Seeing more than one point of view, even just as a reaction, represents a tiny movement toward branching, the first step of IC. We often see other viewpoints only in caricature or overly simplified, mainly denying their legitimacy. But however dismissively we see that other viewpoint, seeing it at all represents a step in the right direction. It is the very beginning of thinking in a transformative way.

> Friend M: You really hurt my feelings. I trusted you. I was telling you something that was close to my heart and you just tuned me out. Why do you pretend to be interested when you are not?
>
> Friend N: I do care. I was listening. I just don't have anything to say.
>
> M: What do you mean you don't have anything to say? I've just poured my heart out and you don't have anything to say?
>
> N: I don't know what to say!
>
> M: How can you not know what to say?! Forget it. I don't want to talk about it any more.
>
> N: I don't have to know what to say. I don't have to say anything. You're the one with the problem.

M recognizes N's point of view but doesn't think it's legitimate. Even so, M has taken a tiny step toward a higher IC level. It doesn't look like it from the exchange of words, but it's part of branching, the first step of IC.

Very, very few people look at conflicts from different angles, granting validity to other points of view despite disagreement. One study found that only 20 per cent of a group of self-identified liberal and conservative Christians looked at a moral dilemma from different points of views.[17] Importantly, the 20 per cent who did so were from across the theological spectrum. No initial position or viewpoint is predisposed to seeing other points of view: it is difficult for all of us. Another study found that thirty senior church leaders across six denominations did not look at a moral dilemma from different points of view. However, with training and visual cues they all learned to see other viewpoints and to integrate them into win–win ways forward.[18] We can learn to transform conflict despite the cumulative trauma of past clashes with our loved ones.

4) The heart v. head in my brain:
A false dichotomy with some usefulness

We all have predispositions or tendencies that steer our responses to the world around us. We rely on our "gut" or our "intellect" to guide us through life.

Tick which applies to you. You might think that both apply, but if you had to choose one, which would you tick?

Do you tend to go with your ☐ heart or your ☐ head when faced with a conflict between the two?

How would you describe yourself: ☐ hot-headed or ☐ coolly rational?

Do you like to work with ☐ images or ☐ words?

To any of these questions, you might be tempted to say, "Well, it depends on the context." And, yes, context affects how we operate. We might have a preferred way of operating regardless of the context, or we might have different preferences for different contexts. Perhaps we've learned to operate a certain way because it was more effective – "safer" even – than our preferred way of operating.

Although each of us is a combination, most of us will lean toward one end of this continuum:

"Heart"	"Head"
Emotional	Rational
Intuitive	Analytical
Experiential	Theoretical
Images, symbols	Words

Thoughts and feelings are intertwined – we feel passionate about our cause and think deeply about a particular feeling such as love – yet most people struggle to integrate "head" and "heart".[19] Someone who fears their emotions or has not learned to value them will struggle to stay with their feelings, to name them, and to process or reflect on them enough to understand their own viewpoint. In contrast, someone who doesn't like to over-think or was not encouraged to problem-solve will struggle to think about a conflict long enough to consider different points of view. It takes intentional focus and support to take in what is going on around us in a way that integrates our feelings and thoughts, especially in the heat of a conflict.

Women v. men: A false dichotomy without usefulness
The stereotype is that women are led by their hearts (left side of the continuum) and men by their heads (right side of the continuum).[20] This has been reinforced by the colloquial phrase "Men are from Mars, women are from Venus" and the popular books using this phrase.[21] However, research has found that men and women are both from Earth![22] There are greater differences among women and among men than between men and women. Cultural expectations and upbringing seem to have more influence on a person's development than their gender. Even with so-called "gendered traits", such as spatial awareness and empathy, there is less difference between the genders than there is within the genders. "So it is misguided at best – and deceptive at worst – to make pronouncements about 'gender essentials' when much more variability exists *within* than *between* the sexes, and when even the remaining differences are unstable!"[23] Clashes between men and women are not so much about gender differences as about human differences – and similarities.

Our family's, school's, and voluntary organization's or faith community's attitudes toward how men or women "should" behave during conflict shape our reactions to conflict. Family messages can discourage healthy and creative conflict with words such as "Just keep your head down and mind your own business – you're lucky you have a roof over your head". Our faith community might send the message that conflict is "un-spiritual" with words such as

"We need to be in unity on this and if you disagree, you need to think about going somewhere else". Critical assessment or evaluation might be considered un-spiritual – "Everyone is trying so hard, we need to show our appreciation and not be critical."[24] In Chapters 3 and 6, reflection about childhood experiences of conflict is suggested. We are shaped by a cocktail of influences so that some conflict behaviour is considered good (perhaps avoidance or denial) and other conflict behaviour is considered bad (perhaps even *acknowledging* conflict).

This cocktail of influences (individual, familial, social, cultural, religious) will not permit us to see any other viewpoint without great effort and practice. If we tend toward being more analytical, and our family and faith community insist that unity means dispensing with questions and critical evaluation, then we will feel as if we cannot be ourselves. A taboo for women against what is perceived as "unladylike negativity" will leave critically thinking women feeling like misfits. If we tend to be emotional, and our school and work say we have to be coolly rational to get on, then we will feel unable to be ourselves. The framework of IC embraces and integrates head and heart reflection as essential for seeing our own and others' viewpoints.

5) The left brain v. right brain:
A false dichotomy with some usefulness

Our entire brain is always active, but our preference for certain types of experiences and ways of processing information (for example, through our senses or intuition) means that parts of our brains become more proficient.[25] As we use those parts of our brains more, they become yet more proficient. This ongoing development of specialized functions has entered into common parlance with talk about being left- or right-brained. Of course, none of us is left- or right-brained, unless our brains are damaged, but this colloquialism arose from linking personal tendencies with brain functioning in each hemisphere.

Travelling down an urban street or a village high street, do you notice the details (the architectural changes, the colours in the window displays, the shoes or handbags of other pedestrians, the wording and lettering style of signs) or the big picture (that you're in a crowd or relatively alone on the pavement, that there are buildings around you or you're in an open space, that it's bright out or cloudy)?

Perhaps you notice both. Many, however, will recognize themselves as very definitely one or the other. If you had to choose one, would you say you focus on details or the big picture?

Next, think of a recent argument or conflict with someone. Did you focus on the details or on the overall theme of the conflict? (There is more on this in Chapter 4.)

The following diagram indicates some specializations in our brains:

Left-brain functions		Right-brain functions
Analytic	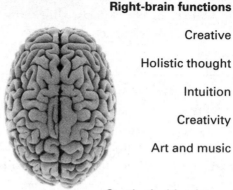	Creative
Analytic thought		Holistic thought
Logic		Intuition
Language		Creativity
Science and mathematics		Art and music
Detailed analysis:		Synthetic, big picture:
Figure *or* ground		Figure *and* ground

All three layers of the brain – the inner brain stem, the middle limbic system, and the outer neocortex – are divided into these two hemispheres.

The whole brain
In conflict, the limbic system of a person with left-brain dominance will express anxiety with logical arguments and detailed analysis. The limbic system of a person with right-brain dominance will have a holistic sense about the situation but may not be able to articulate it very well. The first person can marshal their verbal arguments in support of their viewpoint, annoyed that the other can't say what they mean. The second person doesn't state their view very clearly and can't understand the other's barrage of words, but knows they strongly prefer their own viewpoint. The two people are stuck.

Husband: Let's do something relaxing this weekend. I'm bushed.

Wife: I'm tired too, but we need to get some things done as well.

Husband: Oh no, not another laundry list of errands.

Wife: The refrigerator is empty, the printer is out of paper – and so are the toilets! – and it's your mother's birthday next week.

Husband: There goes the weekend.

Wife: I want a break too, but you'll be the first to complain if we don't have anything to eat.

Husband: Forget it. I was just hoping we could have some fun for once.

Wife: I want fun too. Why am I always the bad guy? Why can't we work together on this and have fun while we're doing it?

Husband: Gee, great. Fun in the grocery store. (Turns on the television.)

Wife: Stop being a baby. That's not what I meant and you know it. Who could have fun with you anyway? (Walks out of the room.)

The wife is able to state her viewpoint clearly and in detail, but the husband feels overwhelmed and shuts down. The wife doesn't understand what her husband is trying to say. They are isolated from one another, unable to understand the other's point of view, while beneath their words are cries for connection. Their limbic systems have brought their bodies to attention so that their strengths are marshalled for survival. But neither has heard the other and they go away from the conflict alive but alone.

Denying the existence of conflict or thinking that it is possible to avoid conflict does not prevent our brains and bodies from going into high alert. Our physiological and emotional responses tell the story of how we have adapted to survive on planet Earth. But will we survive relationship conflict in the twenty-first century?

The secreting emotions and transference

Maybe the route to bliss involves getting rid of emotions, becoming more rational. What do you think?

Even if it were possible, it wouldn't be a good idea. Without emotions, we are not *able* to function rationally. Emotions provide vital, meaningful information about ourselves, other people, and our world. They enable us to enjoy life in 3-D.[26] All emotions have a cognitive component: emotions make a thought meaningful, important to us; neurologically, we cannot have a thought without emotion. But we can function without emotional *awareness*. And most of us do. Emotional awareness means recognizing our personal signs of stress and tension and taking care. We will pay for emotional *un*awareness through something called "transference".

Transference goes on all the time. It is the process of responding to someone *as if* they were someone else. Usually it is fairly benign, but sometimes it can wreak havoc. Without emotional awareness, we might find ourselves yelling at someone *as if* they were our mother, spouse, close friend, or business partner. To become aware of this unconscious connection, we need to cultivate emotional awareness.

Let's say I'm sitting in a coffee shop reading while enjoying my favourite brew. A woman starts to cough. I feel really annoyed. I wonder why but don't really focus on it. Unconsciously, I look up and send her a cold glance. "Drink some water," I mutter under my breath. I catch myself. This doesn't feel good. I feel anxious and upset and tell myself to get a grip. But I go through the rest of the day irritable and grumpy, responding tersely to my colleagues and then going home.

I start criticizing my spouse about something silly just because I feel out of sorts. I can see what I'm doing but I can't stop myself. My spouse retaliates and a conflict ensues. We go to bed in icy silence, backs turned, or maybe I'm on the sofa.

With emotional awareness, scroll back to the coffee shop. I notice that I'm feeling annoyed, tense, and anxious. I stop reading, take a deep breath, and decide to explore my feelings, asking myself when I first felt annoyed. I trace it back to the woman coughing. That was the trigger. I almost laugh aloud. Why did her coughing so annoy me? What does her coughing remind me of? I have an "aha!" moment. I make the connection. Her cough sounded just like my hated teacher who belted (or embarrassed) me every time I got a maths problem wrong. I am stunned by the powerful sensations of my feelings. That cough took me right back to those days of agony. I sit for a few minutes with the memory of that teacher and my experiences in her classroom. They were awful. Humiliating. She was wrong to do that. I remind myself that I'm not that child any more. I'm an adult who would walk away from that sort of treatment.

I take a deep breath and return to the present, looking at the report or magazine lying next to my coffee cup. Perhaps I'll journal about my experiences or confide in my close friend or partner. Perhaps I'll meditate or pray about it and talk with a counsellor, mentor, or spiritual friend. My emotional awareness has enabled me to stay connected with myself and with those around me rather than led to destructive behaviour. The original conflict with my hated teacher was traumatic, but my willingness to face a painful memory has led to emotional awareness and growth, instead of morphing into another conflict with my colleagues and spouse.

What if my emotional awareness comes later? I'm on the sofa, wondering what went wrong. I go through the same process, tracing my annoyance back to the cough, images of the hated teacher, and so on. What I do with my discoveries is critical. Using the framework of IC, it will involve listening as well as speaking.

Ultimately, we pay for a lack of emotional awareness with our well-being. We feel as if we're having a heart attack and find ourselves hooked up to machines in hospital. Then we listen to a doctor telling us about panic attacks and how they mimic the symptoms of heart attacks. We start to show the symptoms of post-traumatic stress. Life feels overwhelming. We want to hide.

Self-awareness

Our limbic system puts our body on red alert *with merely the anticipation or expectation of conflict, even a minor one.*[27] It also has a memory. If a current situation feels familiar, like something unpleasant we've been through before, then without emotional awareness the stress of the past will compound the stress of the present. To overcome the five brain challenges to higher IC and conflict transformation, we have to pay attention to the reactions of our body and emotions and cultivate emotional awareness.

How does *your* body signal that you are stressed and anxious? Reading this chapter might have elicited some physical reactions in your body.

Check in with your body. The following bodily experiences are all common signs of stress or anxiety. They might indicate that your limbic system is anticipating or expecting conflict. It is sending panic signals through your body and the result is these physiological expressions of stress.

What is going on?

- ❑ palms sweaty?
- ❑ heart pounding?
- ❑ hands shaking?
- ❑ voice pitched higher than usual?
- ❑ mouth dry?
- ❑ hands in fist?
- ❑ jaw clenched?
- ❑ eyes filling with tears?

Recognizing these signals enables you to take steps to calm yourself. Remind yourself that your body will relax when it feels safe. You can help your body feel safe with some simple exercises.

Read through the following and tick the ones that sound like they might be helpful for you. You might find that being mindful, contemplative, or praying while doing any of the following increases your sense of safety:

- ❑ breathe deeply
- ❑ get up and stretch
- ❑ close eyes
- ❑ describe in writing the source of your stress

☐ walk around the room   ☐ walk down the corridor

☐ walk through a green   ☐ walk around the block
　space

☐ drink a glass of water   ☐ look at a peaceful
　　　　　　　　　　　　　　　photograph

☐ light a candle   ☐ read a favourite passage
　　　　　　　　　　　　　　　or poem

☐ listen to a piece of music ☐ other: _____

☐ draw or sketch

Be aware of your bodily sensations when you do anything that you have ticked above. Some sensations you might notice include slower breathing, relaxed muscles, unlocked jaw, open hands, and so on.

Take a moment to contrast the bodily sensations you feel when anxious with the bodily sensations you feel when calm. The two steps of IC will be easier after you've slowed down, shifting your body into a calmer state. You'll know you've done this by the change in your body's sensations.

*

Perhaps you've remembered a hurtful experience. You don't need to fear your hurtful memory. You can try an exercise that might help you to feel the feelings in a safe way and help you to move forward. The same exercise can be really helpful if you anticipate or are currently in a conflict with someone. It's called the empty chair exercise:

Place an empty chair in front of you. Imagine that the person who hurt you in the past, with whom you are in conflict, or with whom you anticipate a future conflict is sitting in the chair. Think for a moment about what you would like to say to them. Then say it aloud. Address the chair as if the person were there in front of you. You might begin with "What I really want to say to you is…" Shouting, crying, anything is allowed. When you are finished, reflect on how you feel. You might want to note something down in a journal.

When ready, think about what you would like to hear the person say in response. In an ideal world, what are/were you longing to hear from your conflict partner? When ready, say it aloud. You might begin with "What I really long(ed) to hear you say is…" When you are finished, notice how you feel. Again, you might like to write it down. When ready, you might like to acknowledge what you have done – by going for a walk, spending some time in meditation or prayer, listening to some music, or doing something else that honours the courage you have just shown.

Some people prefer to do the empty chair exercise in the presence of another trusted person – a counsellor, spiritual director, life coach, mentor, close friend or spouse. If the person is not trained (for example, a friend or spouse), then ask them just to sit with you but not to interrupt or involve themselves, except perhaps to hold your hand as a supportive gesture and/or pray silently.

Other-awareness

Sensitized to our own signs of stress or anxiety, we think our friend, business colleague, or loved one seems stressed. Can we help? Telling them that they look stressed or anxious might receive an explosive response: "Of course I am stressed: you won't agree with anything I say!" Similarly, asking them what is wrong might elicit an exasperated "What do you think? I've already told you!" We may not remember what was said or even the topic of disagreement. We could explode in return and escalate the tension in the conflict. Or we might try another strategy.

We can help someone de-stress and lower their anxiety by listening. Listening carefully and reflecting back what we hear them saying will lower their stress and anxiety. This way of listening is called active listening (see Chapter 4). The first invitation in any conflict may be an invitation to listen. That may sound so basic as to be off-putting. But most of us are not good at listening – to ourselves let alone to other people. As we get older, we tend to hear what reinforces our own viewpoint and to dismiss or discount contradictory information, yet this is *not* inevitable. By reading this book, you have already decided to listen to another viewpoint.

CHAPTER 3

My group made me do it

In addition to the five challenges from our brain are five social challenges to conflict transformation.

We like being ourselves, being an "I", and we like belonging to a group, being part of an "us". There's a rush from being part of a group that feels right. And yet we remain different from other people, even when we want to be with them and like them. This human striving to be connected and separate has been told and retold in story after story around the world. It is central to the story of conflict transformation.

Party Pal: Come on. Let's go out. I want to have fun.

Spend Pal: I'm already overdrawn, but who cares? The way things are going, we might all be redundant next week.

Conflicted Pal: Yeah, OK... or, you know what, I don't feel like it. I think I'll stay in.

Spend Pal: Ahh, come on. What's your problem?

Party Pal: Don't be a pain.

Conflicted Pal: No, really, I don't want to. You guys just go.

Spend Pal: I'm sick of this. Don't come, then.

Conflicted Pal: That's what I'm saying.

Party Pal: Look, we're pals, right? We stick together. So we're going out. OK?

Conflicted Pal: Lay off, would you? I don't want to. OK?

Conflicted Pal feels torn between what the group wants to do (go out) and what s/he wants to do (stay in). What happens when your spouse or best friend pressures you to do something you don't want to do?

1) We get lost in the crowd

"Oh, for more community!" goes the lament about selfishness and isolation in our radically individualist culture. There is only "I", with no commitment to "us". Yet societies with a radical communal ethos can foster suspicion and distrust of uniqueness. There is only "us", with no permission for "I". Humans need both individuality and community. Without both, we are vulnerable to groupthink and only a powerful insight can liberate us, as recounted by the British poet Benjamin Zephaniah:

> I'm an Aston Villa fan, but I stopped going to football matches
> for a long time when it got violent – I mean really violent – in the
> late 1970s. I remember once we were chanting and singing going
> to Birmingham's New Street Station because we'd heard there
> were some Manchester United fans there. We were going there to
> fight them, to spill their blood, to do them in. I walked and sang
> with the fans, but then when we had to go past my house I looked

*up and saw my mother looking out. I hid my face so she couldn't
see me. She looked out and saw what she probably thought was
a group of hooligans singing. I looked into myself and thought,
why the hell am I going to meet these people at a train station?
Because they happen to support a different team from me? If I
was born in Manchester I'd probably support Manchester United
too. It was crazy. I turned back and went home and I didn't go
to another football match for almost 20 years. . The songs we
chanted have stayed with me... there's something really tribal
about them. I'm convinced that there's a human need for people to
come together and sing together... When does a community of that
size come together and sing like that? Even churches don't have
those kinds of numbers.*[1]

Zephaniah has two conflicts. Initially, the anticipated violent
conflict at the train station takes centre stage. But with the
appearance of his mother's face, Zephaniah's inner conflict
moves to centre stage and the anticipated fight between
football fans moves to the background. This reversal in focus
– from the conflict between fans to the one inside him –
facilitates the insight that transforms Zephaniah's world. We
catch an inspiring glimpse of how conflict is an opportunity
to learn and grow.

His mother's face triggered Zephaniah's inner conflict
between the expectations and loyalties of his family and his
gang of football fans. You could say he felt a clash of world
views within himself: the violent world view of the gang and
the disapproving world view of his mother. As these views
clashed, he gained clarity on himself, his group, and his
opponents. The conflict between the two views facilitated a
powerful insight, and without that world-view clash he might
be dead.

Even with the world-view clash, it could have turned out differently. Zephaniah could have attacked (the fight response) his mother: "Why is she looking out of the window? What she sees is her problem!" He could have run away (flee): "Nah, that's not her. If it is, she can't see me." He could have shut down (freeze): "I don't see anything. I'm just singing with my mates." Instead, he walks away. He doesn't dehumanize the crowd; he understands the appeal of what they're doing – "there's something really tribal about them. I'm convinced that there's a human need for people to come together and sing together". Instead, he appreciates what is valuable in both views. He integrates his mother's rejection of violence with his gang's sense of community, becoming both connected and separate.

Zephaniah got lost in the crowd. He could have found himself crying, "My group made me do it!" But he finds himself just in time.

When did you last feel lost in a crowd? Did you do anything you regretted?

When did you last feel torn between what someone you cared about wanted you to do and what you wanted to do? What happened?

We wear a mask

When we're lost in the crowd, being connected means wearing a mask. But we don't only wear masks when we get lost in the crowd. Completely alone, I can have an inner conflict between my real or true self and my false self. My true self is angry and grumpy, while my false self is smiling and saying everything is fine. Which self will I be? Will I keep the mask on, maybe watch television, drink until I fall asleep; will I take it off, try to understand why I feel angry and grumpy, perhaps journalling or listening to music?

Our false self (our mask) appears in response to social experiences. Our groups teach us when to put the mask on and off. Perhaps one of our groups (familial, social, professional, recreational, or religious) frowns on anger and grumpiness, so up goes the mask. But we may be tired of holding up the mask, pretending we don't feel the way we do. It starts to slip.

Wearing masks sabotages self-awareness. When we provoke a conflict because we're feeling grumpy, masks block our way back to the true source of our grumpiness. Paying attention to our inner conflicts can help us to lower the mask.

The challenges of getting lost in the crowd and the pressure to don a mask of whatever is deemed acceptable doesn't mean that groups are inherently bad. The civil rights, anti-apartheid, and environmental movements are groups of people gathered to work for the common good. Youth groups such as the Scouts can pressure us positively to pick up litter, to tell the truth, or to help someone in need. There is power in numbers, and groups have made our lives better. The pressure of labour unions reduced a legal working day from twelve to eight hours. The advocacy of abolitionists succeeded in making slavery illegal. (Alas, both laws are still violated.) The key is not letting the power of the group turn life into a masquerade.

From "freeze, flee, or fight" to "focus and listen"
Taking off our masks involves listening to ourselves. Family

members, close friends, and relationships with skilled people such as counsellors, spiritual directors, life coaches, and mentors can help us listen to ourselves. By "mirroring" or reflecting back what they hear us say, we hear ourselves. Maybe we didn't say exactly what we meant, but we relax when we feel heard and engaged. With practice, we can learn to replace "freeze, flee, or fight" with "focus and listen" – to ourselves and others.

Reflective listening is a core skill for conflict transformation (see Chapter 4). A lack of mirroring, of not being seen or heard, leads to trauma and the slow disintegration of a person's self. In Chapter 2, we described the self-perpetuating and mutually reinforcing cycle of conflict and trauma. Children and adults often prefer negative attention to no attention. They are fighting against the annihilation of invisibility. The stress of job loss and homelessness involves an encroaching sense of being invisible. If no one seems to see me, do I exist? A life-giving aspect of faith bestows a sense of being seen by God.

Mr Squirrel's Nursery in Edinburgh[2] teaches toddlers the building-block skills for active listening. Here are some of the questions used to develop reflective skills:

• You seem very happy now. Can you explain why?

• I can see you are angry. Can you use words to explain to your friends why you are so angry?

• What does your friend's face say to you? (He is sad because I took his toy.)

• What expression does this person have on their face? How do you think they feel?

These toddlers are learning what it feels like to see and be seen. Primed for IC, allowed to have their own viewpoint and to see the viewpoints of others, they can be connected and separate.

We want to be connected (in relationship) with a friend or colleague but also free to be ourselves. We love our partner but we also need time with other people and alone. The desire to be connected and separate starts from when we are very young and features in conflict until we die. We get stuck in symbiosis.

Symbiosis involves the use of other people to serve ourselves. For example, a baby might see the mother or carer as an extension of themselves, rather than a separate person. As adults, we operate out of symbiosis in subtle and not so subtle ways. A parent pressures a child to behave in a particular way so that the parent feels good about themselves. The child feels unaccepted for who they are and conflicted about pleasing their parents. The parent reassures themselves that they are exerting pressure for the child's own good. It takes a brave and wise parent to examine motives honestly and to parent in a way that allows for the uniqueness of the child while setting appropriate boundaries.

Some who study infant behaviour see it as "proto-empathic", with an incipient awareness in the infant of connection and separation between themselves and other people.[3] A baby may need to be supported in maintaining and developing this "connected and separate" way of being with other people, rather than learning how to do it from scratch. "From the beginning, the newly conceived infant has some awareness of the otherness of the 'other', there is never absolute psychic symbiosis"; and equally, there is never total differentiation – we always have some sense of connection.[4]

Wherever we start, most of us move into symbiosis. And conflict follows. We use other people to serve ourselves, even those we love. When we fight with those we love, we objectify or dehumanize them in the service of our viewpoint, becoming so self-absorbed that we see them in ways that reinforce our perspective. Our sense of self, of who we are, and of how the world works, depends on guarding our view of "how things are". When that is threatened, we panic.

Ginger: Hello, Janet's Daughter. I like your nail varnish. Great colour.

Janet's Daughter: You should. It's yours. I found it in your cupboard upstairs. (Walks out.)

Janet: Isn't that sweet?

Ginger: Hmm. Is that usual?

Janet: What?

Ginger: Your daughter going through other people's cupboards and helping herself?

Janet's friend Merrin: What do you mean? I'm sure Janet's Daughter thought she was welcome to make herself at home here. We're all such good friends.

Ginger: Yes, but I'd ask for permission before I used something of yours.

Janet: Well, I'm certainly not so precious about my things. What's mine is hers. She's my mini-me. You should feel flattered. She already feels comfortable with you and likes your taste.

Merrin: Really, Ginger, I do think you're being unreasonable.

Janet: I think you are. Two against one.

Merrin and Janet are feeling threatened as their friend Ginger challenges their views about close relationships and parenting. Janet seems glued to her daughter: "What's mine is hers. She's my mini-me." In contrast, Ginger is trying to be both connected and separate: "Yes, but I'd ask for permission before I used something of yours." In this clash of world views among friends, Ginger feels invaded, whereas Janet and Merrin feel pushed away. Asserting the superiority of their enmeshed world view and in-group, Janet argues, "Two against one – we think you are unreasonable." Enmeshment (rather than isolation) seems to be on the rise as Baby Buster parents react against the emotionally reserved parenting they experienced from their Baby Boomer parents. We revisit parenting styles in Chapter 6. At stake is the next generation's ability to be connected and separate with their loved ones.

2) Our loved ones become enemies

In any conflict between two people, the source of the conflict goes beyond the individuals; it includes the social world of the conflict partners, their loyalties to family, culture, religion, politics. When embroiled in a conflict with someone who is part of a group we oppose, the dispute is not just between my conflict partner and me, it's between our groups and our world views too. Individuals and communities interpenetrate. We don't get one without the other. The most painful conflicts involve clashes between the world views of different groups, represented by the two angry people facing each other.

This division of people into in-groups and out-groups holds true across generations, cultures, and genders. Even in a group with no history, without knowing the identity of the other people in our in-group, we do whatever it takes to put our own group at an advantage and the out-group at a disadvantage.[5] We automatically favour our own group over every other group, even we seek to cloak that with politeness. Women are not any cattier than men; we all put down or speak critically about our out-group. Conflict arises not only between groups but when people shift between groups, in or out. Movement in either direction can turn loved ones into enemies.

Movement between groups: You're out!
When someone we care about, whether a close colleague or a life partner, moves from our in-group to our out-group, they become "the enemy".

> He: I thought you loved me.

> She: I do. I just don't agree with you.

> He: If you loved me, then you would agree with me.

> She: What are you talking about? Of course I love you. I just don't agree with you on this topic.

> He: This topic means a lot to me and no one who really loves me would disagree with me on it.

> She: This is ridiculous. I'm not continuing this. (Walks away.)

> He: See. This is the beginning of the end. A couple has to agree on everything if they're going to stay together. (Sigh) I thought she loved me.

The topic being disputed might concern politics, morals, art, faith… you name it. Underneath the difference of opinion lies a clash of views on the nature of love. He thinks love means being connected without any differences. She thinks love means being connected and separate. Because she disagrees with him, she has moved from his in-group to his out-group. Her different view of love threatens his view of how the world works. And how we see our world makes us who we are. So, in a world-view clash, we can feel like our very identity, our very self, is under attack. In response, the limbic system activates the five brain challenges to conflict transformation. He sees *only* his own point of view.

It is true that this world-view clash could trigger greater clarity in the relationship. Those in the conflict could raise their IC levels; they could build on their shared value of love until they are able to weave together their opposing views on love. Instead, their mutual cry is "You're out!"

Movement between groups: You're in!
Have you ever been intentionally helped by an enemy, a member of your out-group? If you have, then you know how disconcerting it can be. We struggle to take it in. The old categories are not working any more. We feel shaken. We ask ourselves, "If that person helped me, then are they now my friend? And if they're my friend, then who is my enemy? Where do I fit in? What will my loved ones think?"

When a "good cop" and "bad cop" interrogate someone and then switch roles, they hope to take advantage of the confusion and distress this movement creates. Not only do our categories about other people shift (who is part of our in- group or out-group), but our own identity (which is partly based on the categories making up our world view) can start to crumble. This is very distressing, activating our limbic system to send out red-alert signals. Our brain resists this shift in categories. Moving beyond binary thinking, transcending our categories of friend and foe, in-group and out-group, is stressful, even when the news is good – we have a new "loved one" – because we also have new enemies. Our loved ones may now distrust us.

The title of the story "The Good Samaritan" might today be somewhat akin to "The Good Terrorist". It concerns a man who is helped by his out-group, his enemy, after members of his in-group choose not to help him. It begins with a verbal joust.

Looking for a loophole, a religious scholar asked, "And just how would you define 'neighbor' "?

Jesus answered by telling a story. "There was once a man traveling from Jerusalem to Jericho. On the way he was attacked by robbers. They took his clothes, beat him up, and went off leaving him half-dead. Luckily, a priest was on his way down the same road, but when he saw him he angled across to the other side. Then a Levite religious man showed up; he also avoided the injured man.

"A Samaritan traveling the road came upon him. When he saw the man's condition, his heart went out to him. He gave him first aid, disinfecting and bandaging his wounds. Then he lifted him onto his donkey, led him to an inn, and made him comfortable. In the morning he took out two silver coins and gave them to the innkeeper, saying, 'Take good care of him. If it costs any more, put it on my bill – I'll pay you on my way back.'

"What do you think? Which of the three became a neighbor to the man attacked by robbers?"

"The one who treated him kindly," the religion scholar responded.

Jesus said, "Go and do the same."[6]

The Samaritan overcomes the stress of his default social setting (in-group, out-group) with an empathic response to his "enemy". He has a new "loved one". He even thinks past the immediate need, enabling the innkeeper to do whatever is necessary to help the hurt man. Good thing, too. The Jewish man needs time to recover not only from his injuries but from the shock of having his world view, his very identity, shaken. A member of his *out*-group has rescued and generously cared for him. Saying to the Samaritan, "You're in!" has consequences. The Jewish man's in-group is not going to like it (after all, they didn't help him and won't like being shown up by an enemy). We all need time to think that one through. But this story is from an ancient world. We're more enlightened now, right?

British actor and writer Alexei Sayle describes moving away from in-group/out-group thinking after the fall of the Berlin Wall. The economic and philosophical system that his parents had fought for all their lives and that had shaped his own world view had imploded.

The foundations of our global outlook crashed along with the wall… I felt foolish… I felt stupid and guilty watching the happy Ossis [East Germans] streaming through Checkpoint Charlie, because I realized that I'd fallen into the trap that so many on the left constantly fall into.

We want to think that we are on the side of goodness and justice, and can't cope with the moral ambiguities that attend most human affairs. Thus we can find ourselves defending despots, terrifying terrorist groups and plain madmen because they said they were socialists or anti-imperialist or just poor, and we so wanted to believe them, simply because their struggle had begun with a justified impulse…

*... the only way I can make amends for my previous myopia
is to become obsessive in trying never to ignore the deficiencies of
my own argument, and to keep in the back of my mind the idea
that I could always be wrong.*

The consequence is that Sayle is no longer trusted by his in-group. He is no longer a "loved one" within his own group.

*Those whose causes I support sigh when I turn up at a rally or
press conference, and they would much rather have me on the
other side, since I'm constantly saying confusing things and
agreeing with my opponent. But I hope in the end it is more
important to do that than to resort to bombast and sloganising.*[7]

Overcoming the default setting of his brain that insists on creating in-groups and out-groups – and starting to integrate opposing viewpoints – has cost Sayle time, effort, and love. A sequel to the Good Samaritan story might feature the helped man facing his in-group's protests that a member of his out-group saved him. Would they prefer that he had died? Well, whatever it takes to uphold the group's binary viewpoint! Movement between groups in either direction, even without any intentionality on our part (the Samaritan helps the hurt Jewish man while he's unconscious), can turn our loved ones into enemies.

Has a loved one ever become an enemy when you
realized you had different views on an important topic?
What did you do? Are you still in relationship?
Has an enemy ever helped you? How did you feel? How

did other people react? What did you do? Are you now friends?

Has someone close to you been helped by an enemy? How did you feel about it? How did they feel about it?

Eyes of love and hate

Throughout history, in-group/out-group dynamics have pitted brother against sister, husband against wife, aunt against uncle, cousin against cousin, child against parent. The genocide in Rwanda is just one of the more recent examples. We may think we are different. Every person willing to speak about what happened there says the same thing. Except for the evidence before them, they would not believe that their loved ones – neighbours, fellow church members, even family members – could become hated ones. It seems incomprehensible, but the same capacity is inside each of us. Learning to overcome our default social setting is the only way to guarantee that we will not turn eyes of hate on to those we love.

Having enemies (even if they are former loved ones) can feel more comfortable than not having enemies. We like having clear categories, clear boundaries. We have a visceral reaction against cooperation or collaboration with the "enemy". Some of our students say messing with categories this way is too reminiscent of the Second World War and the hated collaborators who betrayed those who helped Jews escape, or turned Jewish women, men, and children over to the Gestapo for deportation. Collaboration takes us too near appeasement, another hated word from WWII. However, working with our enemies in ways that do not betray our core values humanizes us all. We embrace our shared humanity.

Learning to see and integrate different points of view (IC) can keep our loved ones as loved ones and foster peace with our enemies. The more people practising these skills, the less hate is generated when our loved ones make friends with the enemy and vice versa. The only other option is to let our children and grandchildren continue to turn eyes of love into hate. The tales of *Romeo and Juliet* and *West Side Story* illustrate the risks that transcend class, culture, and time. Audiences always leave the theatre thinking, "I'd be different." We hope, with the strategies in this book, we will be.

Most people identify themselves by age, gender, nationality, religion, city or neighbourhood, hobby, sport team, and occupation. How do you identify yourself?

Now identify your in-groups. With which groups do you most strongly associate?

Now think of those groups with which you would *never* identify yourself. Even the idea makes you slightly tense. These are your out-groups.

Write down both your in-groups and out-groups. For each group, name one reason why it is either your in-group or your out-group.

Now write down the names of your "loved ones". Do they have the same in-groups and out-groups as you? Ask them to answer the in-group/out-group questions you've just answered and compare.

---

3) We do conflict as we experience it

Where do we learn to turn loved ones into enemies? Our first group, our childhood family (or families), plays a huge role in forming who we are and how we behave in conflict.

> Parent: Why do you want to have him over to play? I thought he was mean to you yesterday.

> Child: That was yesterday. Everything is fine today.

> Parent: But why would you want to play with someone who is mean to you?

> Child: They're not *really* mean, and it doesn't matter any more.

> Parent: Well, you were very upset yesterday. I think his parents are too lenient with him.

> Child: So, can I have him over?

> Parent: Only if his parents are willing to bring him over. I'm not going to pick him up or take him home.

> Child: Won't you do at least one or the other?

> Parent: No, I have too much going on and I don't think you should play with someone who upsets you so much.

> Child: OK. I'll ask him if he can come over and if his parents can drive both ways.

In this parent–child conflict, we see some building blocks for conflict transformation. First, both parent and child overcome some of their binary thinking. The parent creates in-groups and out-groups – "Why would you want to play with someone who is mean to you? … I think his parents are too lenient" – but the binary division is not rigid. The parent's limbic system has been on high alert in response to their child being upset, feeling protective and concerned. But now they calm down because the child is no longer upset. Similarly, the child doesn't jump into in-group/out-group thinking, as in "Parents never get it! Only my friends understand me!"

Second, each maintains their position, based on their own values. The parent's underlying value is for the child's welfare in relationships. The parent may be concerned that the child does not allow themselves to be bullied and learns to recognize true from false friends. The parent may struggle to forgive minor offences and implicitly teach their child to demand perfection from relationships. Like most of us, the parent probably has a mixture of motives and feels conflicted, owning some motives and not wanting to admit others. But the parent's care for the child runs throughout. Similarly, the child's words – "That was yesterday… it doesn't matter any more" – reveal a consistent value of the friendship and a (perhaps deeper) desire simply to have someone over to play.

Third, they agree to a solution that integrates their values. Moving beyond strict in-group/out-group thinking, the parent integrates the child's values and desires with parental concern. Similarly, the child suggests a way forward that integrates their own desire with the stated desires of the parent. Neither has been dominated by the default settings of the brain and instead each has been able to learn through the conflict. Learning between parents and children doesn't mean that parents become their child's "friend". Rather than enmeshing – getting lost in a crowd of two – and putting on a mask, they are connected and separate. We will return to parenting in Chapter 6.

The first place we learn about conflict is in our families and it starts with the cultivation of empathy.

Empathy: It's a group thing

Our brain requires multiple levels of social interaction to develop fully. For example, unless a toddler experiences considerate behaviour and is gently taught to consider others, their brain's physical structure does not develop the capacity for empathy (earlier than toddlerhood, the brain is not ready to develop empathic structures, although there may be proto-empathic behaviour). The plasticity of our brains (capacity for growth, stretching, and change) means that within certain parameters our social environment continues to form us until the day we die. As older children or adults, we too can develop empathic skills, but it will take time and hard work.[8]

Empathy – the ability to see another's point of view and imagine how they are feeling – is a key skill for conflict transformation. We might continue to disagree strongly, but we understand where they are coming from. Parents have the fun of teaching their children to see and respect different viewpoints, while allowing them to keep their own. If you didn't get this kind of parenting, then it's never too late to reflect on your experience of conflict in your family and to use those insights to plot a way toward becoming more empathic. Without empathy, our IC levels stay low and we continue to clash with everyone who disagrees with us.

- What did I learn about conflict from my childhood family experiences or my cultural group(s)?
- Which ways of handling conflict were not allowed?
- What was allowed or encouraged?
- Is my default conflict style a reaction against what was modelled in my family, or have I followed suit?

---

4) We think it's them or us

A world view is a conceptual framework[9] – like a set of spectacles – through which we view the world and make sense of it. Some people have a very clear idea of their world view; others don't notice their spectacles without someone holding up a mirror. Our world view represents our values, our understanding of how the world works, how we should live in it, and what life is all about. In a world-view clash, there's no coexistence: it's them or us.

As we have described, world-view clashes threaten our identity, how we make sense of the world and who we are. If I am wrong and you are right, then I've been living my life in the wrong way. That's too demoralizing to contemplate, so we want others to admit we are right and they are wrong.

> She: I ought to be able to come home without finding a complete pigsty.
>
> He: (Sigh) There you go. You're barely in the door and those are the first words out of your mouth. Nice to see you too.
>
> She: (Sigh) I'm happy to see you. I'd just like a little consideration. Why can't you leave everything tidy, the way I leave it?
>
> He: Because it's my home. I can relax. Make myself comfortable. It's not a museum, you know.
>
> She: But I've told you a mess makes me feel stressed.
>
> He: And it makes me feel relaxed. Come over here. Relax with me.
>
> She: Ugh. I can't. I'm disgusted.
>
> He: We are *so* different. How did we end up together?

Her conversation starter – "I ought to be able to come home without finding a complete pigsty" – shows that her world view feels under threat. His world view feels threatened too: "It's my home. I can relax. Make myself comfortable. It's not a museum, you know." In this world-view clash, each person feels unacceptable to the other. "How did we end up together?"

The five challenges from the brain swing into action and each person's body goes into high alert. Thinking in binary categories of friend or foe, they see only their own point of view, arguing passionately or spluttering incoherent feelings, getting lost in the details or rambling on about their big vision. In the core of these reactions are deep fears about themselves and their world. "Am I OK? Has my loved one abandoned me? Are they no longer part of my good group? Am I going to have to make it alone? My world is falling apart."

The world according to me: What is a world view?
There are many ways to conceptualize world views. My world view is both descriptive and prescriptive regarding at least seven dimensions of human existence:

1) Human nature
Can we change or are we pretty much stuck with the way we are? Are we by nature pretty good or pretty bad? Are human beings simple to understand or complex?

2) Human will
Are we determined by our biology, by our environment, or can we make our mark on the world using our reason or our intuition?

3) How we think

What are the most important influences – authority, tradition, our five senses, reason, science, intuition, revelation, and so on – and are we the centre of the universe or do we need to transcend our egos?

4) How we should behave

Is it best to be inward- or outward-looking? Focused on the past, present, or future? Try to keep things the same or embrace change? Come up with our own moral code or rely on one that is transcendent?

5) How human and creaturely relationships should be conducted

Is individualism or collectivism best? Are human beings the most important creature on earth or are all creatures valuable? Should we be independent, interdependent, or dependent on one another? Should we embrace cooperation, competition, or disengage from all of that? Should we correct others through rehabilitation or retribution?

6) The nature of truth

Are there universal truths or is truth always relative? Can we perceive the whole truth or is it always partial? Is it available to all or only to some?

7) Our world around us

Is our world purely material or is there a spiritual dimension? Is there a God or is there none? If there is, how involved in the world is God? Is nature conscious or unconscious? Does the universe operate according to a plan or is it purely random? Is the world fair, unfair, or random? Should we be resigned to life or optimistic about it? Is the purpose of life to survive, have pleasure, power, recognition, achieve, actualize, or transcend ourselves? [10]

Phew! A lot goes in to a world view, so a helpful way to start thinking about world views involves just four factors: every world view responds to existential questions about life that weave together to form a narrative or story involving specific practices and symbols that encapsulate and represent the entire world view.

Questions and narrative

Four existential questions focus on meaning and purpose: [11]
  (a) Who are we?
  (b) Where are we? (In what part of the world's big story are we?)
  (c) What is wrong? (However much we appreciate the goodness of the world, there is something wrong; the destruction in the twentieth century nudges if not propels us to that conclusion.)
  (d) What is the remedy?

A "material girl" singing the theme of Madonna's hit song might respond:
  (a) Who are we? We are purely physical beings who should get as much pleasure as possible from the material world.
  (b) Where are we? We are in a material world to meet our needs for limitless physical, material pleasures and infinite possibilities.
  (c) What is wrong? Too few people have enough material pleasure.
  (d) What is the remedy? More people need to acquire more material pleasure: earn more money, buy, spend, accumulate, and enjoy.

How might *you* respond to these questions? Try not to censor yourself or write what you think you should write. Put down what you really think. No one else needs to see what you write and you can put it in a safe place. Consider reviewing it now and again, perhaps on your birthday and each new year.

Competing world views are at war within us all the time, a battle of the false and true selves, our mask and what's behind it. A common inner conflict pits our "goodness" against our "badness":

All good
(a) Who am I? I am good because I do everything just right.
(b) Where am I? I live in the world, which is moving to perfection; my job is to do everything the way it should be done.
(c) What is wrong? The world suffers because people do not do what they should do.
(d) What is the remedy? For all people everywhere to do what they should do.

All bad
(a) Who am I? I am bad and do everything wrong.
(b) Where am I? I live in a world moving towards badness that sees my badness and failings.
(c) What is wrong? The world suffers because I don't get it right.
(d) What is the remedy? To stop doing everything wrong.

These responses weave into different stories or narratives about how the world works. An internal tug of war – a clash of personal narratives – presents us with opposing destinies: self-affirmation versus self-destruction. Some people opt for one or the other, whereas others live on the see-saw of self-care and self-sabotage.

Integrating the "all good" and "all bad" narratives together takes you beyond either into a world view that is broader, deeper, and more nurturing of our *whole* self, the good, bad, and ugly bits. But this process cannot even begin until we see the world-view clash in the first place. Even our inner conflicts are not about us alone. Our conflicts connect us to clashing world views and different groups.

Regardless of the conflict type (inner, interpersonal, between groups), we can integrate the viewpoints, values, and goals of each narrative to transform a world-view clash. A well-publicized narrative clash can take on a life of its own. A lot of press has been devoted to the clash between scientific and religious world view narratives, yet historically they have been mutually supportive more often than not. Beneath the violence of extremist world view narratives (religious, national, secular, and sometimes a toxic cocktail of religious and national), there can be values we all affirm, such as community, integrity, and justice. (For more on conflict transformation with extreme religious views, see Chapter 7.)

Try to weave together into a story your responses to the four existential questions (Who are we/am I? Where are we/am I? What is wrong? What is the remedy?). Write it out and consider reviewing it on days of significance. Over the years, you might notice development of the story.

If you're not entirely pleased with what you've written, then you now know your starting place (your own branch). You can look at other branches and integrate different points of view (weave) to address whatever feels uncomfortable. See a counsellor, spiritual director, mentor, or life coach to support you through the process.

Practices and symbols

Practices make a world view visible in our lives, whether it's putting on an extra sweater instead of turning up the central heating or sending your colleague a postcard every time you go on holiday. Embedded in these practices is your world view, your relationship to the environment or the sharing of holiday experiences. In a faith context, world view practices say that believers live like this, *not* like that. *These* practices indicate you are devout and without them you are not. Without some benchmark practices, however imperfectly lived out, a world view risks becoming disembodied and irrelevant.

Honesty is probably one practice that all world views have as an ideal, even if it is not always fully lived out. We can struggle to be honest with ourselves, let alone with others. Do you think honesty is always the best policy no matter what, or do you think a white lie is OK to protect a loved one's feelings? Any ambivalent feelings might reveal an inner world-view clash. We might have thought this through, integrating aspects from opposing viewpoints into an overall theory about the nature of honesty in various contexts. Is it wrong to lie about a gift hidden from a loved one? Is it wrong to allow a child to deny that their father is a drunk because they don't have the capacity to handle the public shame?

World-view symbols are simple enough to be instantly recognizable, but they enfold an entire world view. For Benjamin Zephaniah, the face of his mother symbolized an entire world view opposing the violent world view of his gang.

World-view symbols can be where we live (for example, our postcode), whether or not we drive a car ("cars are killing the environment" versus "I wouldn't be caught dead on a bus"), where we buy our groceries (only at farmers' markets or only at superstores on sale), or the way we dress (classic, trendy, or who cares?). A single practice can take on symbolic value, representing our world view in one go.

C: Come on. You need to celebrate another year of life.

I: I don't want to. It's just another year closer to death. The less said, the better.

C. I'm sorry, but I'm not going to let you do that. You'll see. You'll enjoy doing something for your birthday and you'd regret not doing anything.

I: Read my lips: N. O. I don't want to do anything. If you organize something, it will be for you, not me. I won't be there.

C: You're so ungrateful. I'm just trying to do something nice for you.

I: Well, do something *I* want, not what you want.

C: Forget it.

I: That's what I said. Forget it.

The practice of birthday celebration versus minimal

acknowledgment can symbolize two different world views about life, death, and the passing of time. This world-view clash is loaded.

5) Our conflicts pile up

Our conflicts are very complicated. The complications have complications and they pile up into three layers (inner, interpersonal, and group).

Inner

When we find ourselves in two minds about something, experiencing an inner conflict, we might think:
- either I'm good or bad
- either God protects me from bad things or God punishes me with bad things.

Try to think of more examples of inner conflicts using "either/or" thinking (or what is technically called "binary" thinking.

Inner conflicts connect with our in-groups and out-groups. If I'm good, then I'm associated with other people and groups that I consider good, an in-group of people who are honest, fair, and treat everyone with respect, for example. If I'm bad, then I'm associated with a group of people I consider bad, possibly people who steal, lie, and hurt others. If God protects me from bad things, then I'm in with the good people whom God loves. If God punishes me with bad things, then am I rejected or loved by God, along with other people I put in either of those categories?

I might oscillate between the poles of each binary thought, but transformation of these inner conflicts will involve an integration of the two opposing views into an overarching understanding. Humanizing the parts of me that I don't like and having compassion for myself, my underlying needs and longings, takes hard work. Counselling, spiritual direction, mentoring, and coaching can help. The value of this work is not just personal. The integrated self-acceptance gained by using IC for inner conflicts lays the foundation for using IC in interpersonal conflicts.

Interpersonal
In the heat of an interpersonal conflict, we might think:
- either my mother is good or she is bad
- either my vision for the future is right and yours is wrong, or vice versa
- either we aim for perfection or we become mired in "anything goes"
- either we focus on the task or get bogged down in the relationship.

Try to think of other examples of binary thinking in interpersonal conflicts.

These either/or statements reveal in-groups and out-groups on more than one level. If my mother is good, then she is a member of that revered in-group of "good mothers"; if she is bad, then she is part of the hated out-group of "bad mothers". This will affect how we feel about our family, our primary in-group, and ourselves. We might fight with our mother night and day, but we will always defend one of our tribe (our in-group). Our mother is part of us and we are predisposed to be loyal to her, even when she harms us, although we feel conflicted about her. As children, we condemn our conflicted feelings and blame ourselves for her bad behaviour, all creating more inner conflicts that play out in interpersonal conflicts. (The same dynamics can play out about our father or other primary carers.)

Similarly, if my vision is right, then I'm part of the esteemed, clear-sighted, wise in-group, and you are not. If I aim for perfection, then I'm part of the hard-working and responsible in-group. (On the other hand, my in-group might be the more laid-back brigade who thinks that "anything goes" is its own perfection.) Maybe my in-group is relationally-orientated people who get tired of task-orientated types who are disinterested in people. (Or my in-group is task-focused people who get tired of touchy-feelies who ignore the task.)

I might vacillate between these views, depending on the context and other factors. Using IC means integrating the two opposing views into an overarching perspective. My mother has some strengths and weaknesses; she did her best but was very limited in some ways. I can take what was good from her and be wiser from her mistakes and problems to be my own person, no longer seeing women as potentially harmful and seeing myself as part of a "bad family". If we don't deal with these inner and interpersonal conflicts, group conflicts spring like acorns that grow into big oak trees.

Intergroup
Intergroup conflict might lead to these thoughts:
  • My group is right and yours is wrong.

- Teachers are honest and compassionate whereas bankers are corrupt and out of touch.
- All atheists are good and religious people are bad.

Try to think of additional examples of binary thinking in group conflicts.

If my group is right, then I am right and all my friends are right. Our rightness increases by association. In contrast, the other group's wrongness means they are wrong, and together their whole group is *very* wrong. We tend to have a more complex understanding of our in-group than of our out-group, so we acknowledge complexity in our in-group's "rightness" while seeing the out-group as simply all wrong.[12]

Transforming these conflicts involves integrating the opposing points of view – particularly the positive values underlying the different viewpoints – into a larger perspective that honours the key values of each group. The result is not a muddy compromise (or appeasement) but a way forward that is win–win, good for both parties. It will require listening to the out-group – the hated bankers or religious people – to humanize us all.

The social dimensions of interpersonal conflict often go unrecognized. When we do see them, we feel stuck. How can we possibly transform conflicts that look as if they're just between two people but are really between two groups or even several groups? It's all too complicated and overwhelming. Is there any hope? Yes, we have now faced the two forbidding walls between us and conflict transformation. We do not need to blame ourselves for limbic reactions to conflict. Without them we might not be here because our ancestors probably wouldn't have survived. We do not need to blame ourselves for our social reactions to conflict. They've enabled human survival too. Free of the snares of self-blame and shame, we can learn how to be a peacemaker. Help is actually stretched over the walls, meeting us right where we are and offering a way forward. All we have to do is turn the page...

CHAPTER 4

Peacemaking armoury: Tools, strategies, skills

We have just faced ourselves. Our biological and social reactions to conflict have been helpful in the distant past, but now they are a liability. They form a wall between us and the potential transformation conflict offers. The good news is that we are not trapped. Our secret weapon, IC or "I see!" (branching and weaving), gives us concrete steps for transforming our natural reactions to conflict into a stepping stone for growth. We can already see life on the other side.

In this chapter we go through the nitty-gritty of conflict transformation. We define transformation as being able to ascend the seven levels of IC through branching and weaving – seeing different perspectives and weaving them together into win–win solutions. We think of IC as a continuum:

Level 1	Level 3	Level 5	Level 7
One point of view	Several points of view no integration	Several points of view *some* integration	Many points of view integrated into a win–win solution
No branching	Branching	Branching	Much branching
No weaving	No weaving	*Some* weaving	Much weaving

Before working through this chapter, we're probably at Level 1. Afterwards, we will have what we need to reach Level 7.

The following overview introduces how the tools, strategies, and skills in this chapter work together to help us see different points of view, even those with which we disagree, and to integrate them into a win–win solution. Each italicized phrase identifies a tool we will learn to put into practice.

Consulting the *A to Z of IC*, we start with branching. Step 1a of branching begins right where our two feet are planted. Using *slow and prime*, simple steps to slow down our limbic system and prime our bodies, minds, and hearts for peacemaking, we set in motion the work of conflict transformation. We will use these steps over and over.

Stretching over the wall – the physiological and social obstacles to conflict transformation – is a branch. This is *our* branch: our viewpoint, our values, our feelings and thoughts about a particular conflict. We grab hold, swing on, and follow it over the wall. We use what we have learned about ourselves through two *self-discovery quizzes* and the *Big 5 lenses* to recognize aspects of the conflict that reflect different ways of seeing the world, styles of responding to conflict and differences of opinion, and personality differences, and to remind ourselves of the practical steps we can take to work with our conflict partner.

Step 1b of branching involves looking around and noticing the other branches. None is as strong or carries such lush foliage as our branch (our view on the conflict), but the tree does have other branches. We can congratulate ourselves. We have just made a tiny movement toward conflict transformation: we see that other perspectives exist. They are not as valid as ours, but they exist. Holding on to our branch, we can examine other branches as carefully as we examine our own. What seems really important to our conflict partner(s)? Are there any positives to the other viewpoint(s)? We draw on the *self-discovery quizzes* and *Big 5 lenses* again to think about how our conflict partner sees the world and their style of responding to differences of opinion. We deploy our *active listening* skills so that we can really hear their point of view, while maintaining our own viewpoint. We take stock of the conflict by employing *conflict levels* to assess the tension level and ways to lower it.

Step 2 – weaving – picks up where branching leaves off. We've seen our own and the other branches on the tree and we're feeling faint. This conflict tree is big! To steady ourselves we take hold of different parts of each viewpoint and weave them into something new, something not considered or seen before. We don't eliminate the oppositions between the points of view – the tree still has several branches – but we integrate the differences into a way forward that respects what is most important to us and our partner, family member, friend, or colleague. We try two routes to leverage ourselves to a IC level 7 solution, following the suggestions in *how to weave win–win solutions*.

Branching and weaving turn the tree of conflict into the

tree of life. Using the framework of IC, two steps supported by practical tools, strategies, and skills, we can actually see life flow into the relationship as our perception goes up the seven levels of IC.[1]

After learning the tools, strategies, and skills, *A to Z of IC* draws it all together into a peacemaking armoury.

Get through the first ninety seconds of conflict

Conflict strikes. The limbic system urges us to freeze, flee, or fight, and for ninety seconds those impulses are almost irresistible. Branching? Not on your life! We're also feeling the pull and push of our group loyalties. This conflict is not just about us, it's about the world as we know it. Limbic warp-drive can make time stand still. Our brains, bodies, and group loyalties are geared up for survival, even though this is just a disagreement about keeping our home tidy or visiting in-laws. How do we get through those moments and avoid doing something we regret?

First response: Slow and prime

Simple and basic. That's all we can manage in our present state. We don't want to underestimate the power of our brain, body, and group loyalties on high alert. People have been known to remain disengaged, clean frenetically, or rage for hours in response to the limbic system's call to arms. The disagreement starts out about what to do that evening and ends up criticizing each other's family histories and personal hygiene.

> A: You never want to do anything because your family was so narrow-minded – you never learned how to have fun!

> B: Well, your family did anything for a laugh and didn't care if it hurt anyone! Anyway, you're not dressed to go out – you

haven't even showered!

A: Well, you're so paranoid about germs – no wonder your skin is getting all wrinkly, you shower so often.

B: Well, more frequent bathing and some deodorant would not go amiss on you, *my dear*!

The initial trigger is often just an opportunity to vent frustration about other things that are bugging us. And even they are just covers for deeper issues – usually our old friend, the struggle to be connected *and* separate, accepted for who we are without being enmeshed or rejected. Only a simple strategy will take us out of limbic code red. The first-line response for conflict transformation is to slow and prime: slow down and prime our brain and body for conflict transformation. With practice, these steps start to reprogramme our default stress and anxiety reactions.

1. Breathe deeply. In and out. Slowly. We breathe shallowly during conflict, depriving our brains and vital organs of much-needed oxygen. Our neocortex needs us to breathe deeply and slowly to transform conflict. Inhale calm, exhale stress. As we breathe deeply, we can imagine ourselves getting through this conflict feeling good about how we handled the situation. We can close our eyes for a moment, look down, or focus on something that is calming (see 4 below). We can do this even in an open-plan office. The olfactory passages (from our noses) provide a direct route to our deeper, limbic brain; this is why deep breathing *really* does calm us down, in through the nose slowly and out through the mouth slowly; some scents really can have a calming effect, with different people responding to different scents (e.g., sandalwood, frankincense, lavender) Deeply inhaling and slowly exhaling is a key to calming the limbic system.

2. *Ask for time out.* We need space to think creatively, to choose how to respond. Our limbic systems goad us on – Freeze! Flee! Fight! – but we need time to reflect. Ask for an hour, half a day, even twenty-four hours, and use the time to branch and weave, supported by the other five tools. Arrange a time and place to meet with your conflict partner after this time out.

3. *Stand up and excuse yourself for a few minutes.* It may not be possible to get more than that. Walk around the desk, table, sitting room, down the hall, around the garden, around the block, anywhere. Reassuring the other person (people) we'll be back in a few minutes, they won't think we're disappearing. The lavatory is a handy excuse. Physically get a change of view, a change in outlook. Calling to mind our core values in the situation will energize our return: "What really matters to me in this situation?"

4. *Carry a physical reminder to slow down.* A photo, postcard, rock, shell, prayer beads, piece of wood, quotation, handkerchief, key ring, photo on our mobile: select a symbol for slowing and priming. This symbol gives our neocortex something visual to grab on to for slowing down our limbic system. We need something physical; slowing down is not automatic. We often read about the benefits of deep breathing and imagining ourselves handling something in the way we'd like, but we forget to do it. This object becomes a reminder of our commitment to conflict transformation. Changing our symbol every so often will keep the imagery fresh. Perhaps we will choose something to celebrate a conflict that we transformed. We can look at this object even in an open-plan office.

Meditation, mindfulness, contemplation, or prayer can augment any of these steps.

Keeping your body primed

Drink plenty of water and eat "brain food". Keeping healthy snacks in our home, desk, or office, and carrying them in our handbag and/or briefcase means our brain and body are primed for peacemaking. Know where to purchase them, and don't try to fast from water or food during conflict unless you are practised in these ways of fasting. Refined sugar (pastries, confectionery, and cookies) revs us up and drops us with a splat. Instead, eat brain food, such as nuts and raisins, raw vegetables, smoked salmon, hard-boiled eggs, lean chicken, anything with a low GI (Glycaemic Index). Low GI means that our body slowly burns the fuel (glucose) in that particular food so our energy doesn't spike and plummet. Low blood sugar means the neocortex doesn't have the fuel to function well; we are at the mercy of our limbic system. Whole, less processed grains (brown rice, brown bread, or oat cakes) are better than white grains. Our brains use the lion's share of our glucose, so slow-burning fuel is best during conflict.

Another brain food is *Omega 3, 6, 9 fatty acids*. Seeds (sunflower, pumpkin, and flax or linseed), oily fish such as salmon and mackerel, hummus, almonds and walnuts, and wholegrain bread dipped into a high-quality olive oil are good options. The evidence is mounting. The cognitive and behavioural benefits of diets rich in Omega fatty acids – and the problems that accompany diets poor in these nutrients – are recognized.[2]

Take adequate doses of *B vitamins*. The latest research shows we need much higher doses of B vitamins (for example, B 12) than previously realized. Most of us are not very efficient in our absorption of B vitamins from food or in our conversion of the vitamin into a form our body can use. B supplements are needed to augment what we get from food. B vitamins help our body to cope with stress.[3]

These steps don't involve scaling tall buildings. The goal is basic: to get through those first ninety seconds, those first moments. These easy steps are vital.

Now what?
We're feeling calmer now. Phew. But what's next? It's time to start branching. It may not come easily – a lot of people struggle to say what they feel or think in conflict. So branching begins with self-discovery.

Self-discovery quizzes:
Knowing ourselves so we can know our conflict partners
A lot of conflicts feel personal. We think the person is deliberately attacking our viewpoint. In reality, people see the world and respond to conflict in ways that say more about them than about us. We just happen to be the other person in the conflict; we might be anyone and they'd be saying similar things. All of us have default ways of seeing the world and responding to differences in opinion. When we know these default settings for ourselves, then we start to recognize them

in others. We can learn how to work with our differences and similarities with other people to transform conflict rather than feel like every disagreement is a personal attack on us.

Knowing more about how we see the world and respond to disagreement makes space for other people: "This is me, this is how I see this... I wonder what you think and feel?" Feeling more assured in who we are, recognizing our own tendencies and preferences, helps us to relax and be comfortable with the otherness of people we love. A permanent vagueness about ourselves can make us uncomfortable with others who are at ease with themselves ("Oh, she's so sure of herself. Who does she think she is?"), or can make us attach ourselves and try to suck in what we wish we had ("Oh, she's so sure of herself. I want to hang out with her so I can be just like her"). Knowing more about how we see the world, about how we respond to conflict and differences in opinion, will make us more comfortable with ourselves and other people. We offer two self-discovery quizzes that will raise self-awareness in just these areas.

These quizzes do not provide the last word on any of us. Each can stimulate ongoing self-reflection. Some people get stuck in a side street of self-obsession or preoccupation. On a temporary basis, this can be OK to balance years of no self-awareness. The side street leads back to the main road of self-awareness where we connect with other people. But if we stall on the side street of self-obsession, then our friends, a counsellor, spiritual director, life coach, or trusted mentor can help us reconnect with other people. Most of us will enjoy the process of self-discovery in tandem with greater alertness to other people as well.

*Practical or possibility thinker? **"How we see the world" quiz***
Abigail and Donald want to move house. Abigail sees the practical constraints and needs. Donald envisions all the possibilities. It feels personal – "Abigail always opposes my ideas!"; "Donald never thinks practically!" – but it's not. We need both ways of perceiving a situation, a vision and the practical questions. Our loved one might be the same as us – a practical or possibility thinker – but we have different practical concerns, see different possibilities. Again, it's not personal, it's just different ways of looking at the practicalities or different ways of envisioning what's possible.

This self-discovery quiz focuses on different ways of seeing or perceiving the world: do we rely on our intuition (N) or on our five senses (S)? In other words, do we go with our gut or want to hold something in our hands to feel sure about it? Developed by Leslie Francis, a British psychologist specializing in interpersonal differences, this quiz is an adaptation of the Myers-Briggs questionnaire and has a huge database demonstrating its validity and reliability.[4] After taking this self-discovery quiz, we'll consider what might annoy us in people who see the world differently from us – and why we need one another.

1 How do you perceive the world?

Conflict can develop from misunderstandings; we can misunderstand and be misunderstood by people who see the world differently. This questionnaire will help you to think about how *you* perceive the world. After going through the questions below, on the next page you will find scoring instructions, descriptions of the two different ways of seeing the world, how the differences can lead to conflict, and how they can work together.

The following list contains pairs of characteristics. **For each pair, please circle *one* which is *closer* to the real you, even if you feel both characteristics apply to you.** Circle the characteristic that reflects the real you, even if other people see you differently.

Please complete every question.

Do you tend to be more...
interested in facts   OR   interested in theories?

Are you more...
inspirational   OR   practical?

Do you...
prefer to design   OR   prefer to make?

Do you prefer to...
improve things   OR   keep things as they are?

Are you...
conventional   OR   inventive?

Do you tend to be more...
concerned for meaning   OR   concerned about detail?

Do you prefer...
the concrete   OR   the abstract?

Are you more...
imaginative   OR   sensible?

Are you mostly focused on...
present realities   OR   future possibilities?

Are you...
up in the air   OR   down to earth?

Scoring

N = Intuitive   S = Sensing   Number of Ns =   Number of Ss =

Do you tend to be more...	interested in facts	OR	interested in theories?
	S		N
Are you more...	inspirational	OR	practical?
	N		S
Do you...	prefer to design	OR	prefer to make?
	N		S
Do you prefer to...	improve things	OR	keep things as they are?
	N		S
Are you...	conventional	OR	inventive?
	S		N
Do you tend to be more...	concerned for meaning	OR	concerned about detail?
	N		S
Do you prefer...	the concrete	OR	the abstract?
	S		N
Are you more...	imaginative	OR	sensible?
	N		S
Are you mostly focused on...	present realities	OR	future possibilities?
	S		N
Are you...	up in the air	OR	down to earth?
	N		S

Do you have more Ns or Ss? See if the following validates your highest score:

A. When you feel very tired, are you more N or S?

Do you fail to notice things? Begin to lose things? Get basic facts wrong? (N)

OR

Do you fail to see how pieces fit together? Cannot work out what things really mean? Begin to sink under piles of undigested information? (S)

B. Who annoys you more, those different from you or those like you?

Sensing (S) types may experience intuitive (N) types as impractical daydreamers and impossible to pin down to face facts and reality.

Intuitive (N) types may experience sensing (S) types as people who are far too literalistic, materialistic, unimaginative, and dull.

Think of a conflict with a partner, friend, or colleague that involved different ways of perceiving.

How people who see things differently can help one another:

Sensing types can:
- bring relevant facts to the attention of intuitive types;
- encourage intuitive types to read the instructions on the box and the fine print in the contract;
- inject a dose of realism into the dreams cherished by intuitive types;
- keep records and know where things are when intuitive types are likely to lose touch;
- draw the attention of intuitive types to essential details, facts, and data;
- remind intuitive types that life is for living today.

Intuitive types can:
- help sensing types to develop a vision of future possibilities;
- enable sensing types to approach difficulties with new insights;
- encourage sensing types to manage change positively;
- help sensing types to look at old problems in a new light;
- remind sensing types that future possibilities are worth anticipating and working toward.

When have you been helped by and when have you helped a loved one (family member, friend, colleague) who sees the world differently?

Acknowledgment

Francis, Leslie J., "Francis Psychological Type Scales (FPTS)" in *Faith and Psychology: Personality, Religion and the Individual,* Darton, Longman & Todd, 2004.

What do you aim for in conflict? **Conflict style quiz**

Our "conflict style" refers to our goal in conflict: do we aim for fair play (compromise) or to get our own way (direct), to protect the relationship (accommodate) or to be creative (collaborate)? Maybe we just want some time and space to reflect (avoid). Each of these five styles expresses our limbic system reactions to conflict (flee, freeze, or fight).

If we fight for our own viewpoint, then our conflict style might be *directing*: we care deeply about the task or issue and want the relationship to support what we think is right. Freezing might indicate an *avoiding* conflict style: we care so much about the task and the relationship that we become paralysed in indecision until we have time and space to reflect. Alternatively, freezing can lead to an *accommodating* conflict style: we stall on the task or issue until the relationship is affirmed; we want the task or issue to serve the relationship. The two other conflict styles, *compromising* and *collaborating*, can express the fight response. We care deeply about the task and relationship, and fight for either maximum fair play (compromising) or maximum creativity (collaborating). Fairness and creativity can coincide, but if they don't, then a collaborator aims for creativity and a compromiser for fairness.

Avoiding, directing, accommodating, compromising, and collaborating. Each conflict style is appropriate in different contexts, and we might adapt a different style in different contexts. Directors in the office can be accommodators in the home. We might have one default approach: avoid conflict everywhere or die trying to escape! We might have a repertoire of approaches: collaborating in the office, accommodating on our sports team, avoiding at home, directing in our faith community, and compromising with our friends. The point is to know how we react to the stress of conflict, how the context affects our reactions, and to recognize others' conflict styles. It might feel personal when our loved one or colleague avoids the conflict ("They never deal with the issue at hand!") or directs ("They always try to get their own way!") but it isn't. Their approach to conflict is the way they deal with their stress and anxiety, and it is probably what they learned while growing up (see Chapter 6).

All five conflict styles represent a blending of our concerns for the relationship(s) and the task/issue involved in the conflict, with each style expressing a particular recipe or shape of the blend. The following graph shows how each of the five conflict styles blend or integrate our concerns for the relationship and for the task/issue:

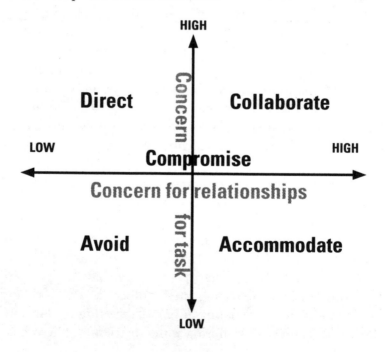

In conflict, we all feel anxious or stressed. Our conflict styles are like mirrors reflecting our behaviour when we feel anxious (when our limbic system is kicking into gear). The questions on this graph help us to get in touch with how anxiety shapes our conflict style.

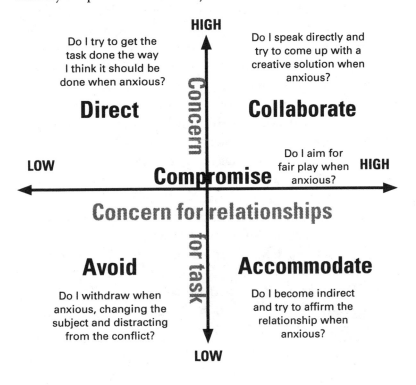

As the questions indicate, when we are anxious, our communication style is affected. We might become very direct in our speech or very indirect. That is, we might beat around the bush, say it like it is, or not say anything at all. How we communicate, how we blend or integrate our concerns for the disputed task with the relationship involved, and what we aim for all come together in our approach to conflict, our conflict style.

The following conflict style quiz was developed by Ronald Kraybill, an international conflict specialist who works at the grass-roots level in hot spots around the world.[5] After going through the quiz, each person has four scores, two referring to their responses to conflict when it is brewing (preferred and back-up calm) and two referring to their responses to conflict when it is raging (preferred and back-up storm). Someone might be an avoider in calm but a collaborator in storm. This means that during the initial stress of conflict, when they can see the conflict brewing on the horizon, they want time and space to reflect. They might seem unaware of the conflict. But when the conflict is raging, in full storm, they directly address the situation, blending their concerns for the relationship and the task/issue in a way that aims for as creative a solution as possible. Without awareness of what they are doing, their switch can alienate people and increase the tension. With awareness, they can choose to switch styles that takes the conflict toward transformation. The scoring key suggests pitfalls and benefits of each conflict style and how to work with them.

2 What is *your* conflict style

In responding to conflict and differences of opinions, you have developed, probably unconsciously, a pattern of behaviour that can be called your conflict style. Different conflict styles work best in different contexts. In learning how to transform relational conflicts, it is important to know what your automatic reaction is likely to be. This exercise will help you to discover that.

Before beginning the questionnaire, think about a recent or present conflict. Try to recall how you felt and what you thought. Think about whether your feelings changed. For example, at first you might have felt like running away and then you felt like fighting. Or perhaps you felt like running away the entire time.

While reading the following statements, think of a recent or present conflict. Bear in mind how your viewpoint was or is different from the other person's.

Statements in Part One deal with your **initial response** to disagreement.

Statements in Part Two deal with your response **after the disagreement has strengthened.**

Please circle the number indicating the extent to which you think each statement describes you.

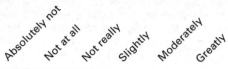

PART ONE

When I *first* discover that differences exist:	Absolutely not	Not at all	Not really	Slightly	Moderately	Greatly
A. I make sure that all views are out in the open and treated with equal consideration, even if there seems to be substantial disagreement.	1	2	3	4	5	6
B. I devote more attention to making sure others understand the logic and benefits of my position than I do to pleasing them.	1	2	3	4	5	6
C. I make my needs known, but I tone them down a bit and look for solutions somewhere in the middle.	1	2	3	4	5	6
D. I pull back from discussion for a time to avoid tension.	1	2	3	4	5	6
E. I devote more attention to the feelings of others than to my personal goals.	1	2	3	4	5	6
F. I make sure my agenda does not get in the way of a relationship.	1	2	3	4	5	6
G. I actively explain my ideas and just as actively take steps to understand others.	1	2	3	4	5	6

	Absolutely not	Not at all	Not really	Slightly	Moderately	Greatly
H. I am more concerned with the goals I believe to be important than with how others feel about things.	1	2	3	4	5	6
I. I decide that the differences are not worth worrying about.	1	2	3	4	5	6
J. I give up some points in exchange for others.	1	2	3	4	5	6
PART TWO If differences *persist* and feelings *escalate*:						
K. I enter more actively into discussion and hold out for ways to meet the needs of others as well as my own.	1	2	3	4	5	6
L. I put forth greater effort to make sure that the truth as I see it is recognized and less effort on pleasing others.	1	2	3	4	5	6
M. I try to be reasonable by not asking for my full preferences, but make sure I get some of what I want.	1	2	3	4	5	6
N. I do not push for things to be done my way, and I pull back somewhat from the demands of others.	1	2	3	4	5	6

	Absolutely not	Not at all	Not really	Slightly	Moderately	Greatly
O. I set aside my own preferences and become more concerned with keeping the relationship comfortable.	1	2	3	4	5	6
P. I interact less with others and look for ways to find a safe distance.	1	2	3	4	5	6
Q. I do what needs to be done and hope we can mend feelings later.	1	2	3	4	5	6
R. I do what is necessary to soothe the other's feelings.	1	2	3	4	5	6
S. I pay close attention to the desires of others but remain firm that they need to pay equal attention to my desires.	1	2	3	4	5	6
T. I press for moderation and compromise so that we can make a decision nd move on with things.	1	2	3	4	5	6

Scoring and interpretation

Transfer the number from each item to the tallies below and on the next page. For example, on item A, if you selected number 6, then write 6 on the line designated for A. Then add the numbers.
Sample: B 1 + H 4 = 5.

This exercise gives you two sets of scores. **Calm** scores apply to your response when disagreement first arises. **Storm** scores apply to your response if things are not easily resolved and emotions get stronger.

The scores indicate your inclination to use each style. The higher your score in a given style, the more likely you are to use this style in responding to conflict. Your highest scores are your preferred conflict styles in calm or storm; your second highest scores are your back-up conflict styles in calm or storm – what you do when your initial efforts fail.

The reflection this inventory can create is more important – and more reliable – than the numbers that the tallies yield. There are no right or wrong answers, nor has the questionnaire been standardized. Some takers agree with the results; others disagree. Whether you like the results or not, you should rely on them for an accurate picture of yourself only after further self-scrutiny and discussion with others. The inventory is a tool to enable these larger tasks.

Styles of conflict management

Collaborating

A _____ + G _____ = _____ Calm
K _____ + S _____ = _____ Storm

You assert your views while also inviting other views; welcome differences; identify all main concerns; generate options; search for a solution that meets as many concerns as possible; and search for mutual agreement.

Perspective on conflict: Conflict is natural, neutral. So affirm differences, prize each person's uniqueness. You recognize that there are tensions in relationships and contrasts in viewpoint. You work through conflicts of closeness.

Compromising

C _____ + J _____ = _____ Calm

M _____ + T _____ = _____ Storm

You urge moderation; bargain; split the difference; find a little something for everyone; and meet them halfway.

Perspective on conflict: Conflict is mutual difference best resolved by cooperation and compromise. If each comes halfway, progress can be made by the democratic process.

Accommodating

E _____ + F _____ = _____ Calm

O _____ + R _____ = _____ Storm

You accept the other's view; let the other's view prevail; give in; support; acknowledge error; or decide it's no big deal/does not matter.

Perspective on conflict: Conflict is usually disastrous, so yield. Sacrifice your own interests, ignore the issues, put relationships first, keep peace at any price.

Avoiding

D _____ + I _____ = _____ Calm

N _____ + P _____ = _____ Storm

You delay or avoid response; withdraw; become inaccessible; divert attention.

Perspective on conflict: Conflict is hopeless, so avoid it. Overlook differences, accept disagreement, or get out.

Directing

B _____ + H _____ = _____ Calm

L _____ + Q _____ = _____ Storm

You control the outcome; discourage disagreement; insist on your view prevailing.

Perspective on conflict: Conflict is obvious; some people are right and some people are wrong. The central issue is who is right. Pressure and coercion are necessary.

Preferred and back-up styles

Using your scores, list your score numbers and style names below in order of largest number to smallest.

The style that receives the highest score in each of the columns – calm and storm – indicates a preferred or primary style of conflict management. If two or more styles have the same score, they are equally preferred. The second highest score indicates one's back-up style if the number is relatively close to the highest score. A fairly even score across all of the styles indicates a "flat profile". People with a flat profile tend to be able to choose easily among the various responses to conflict.

Styles in calm and storm

Calm

Response when issues/conflicts **first** arise

Storm

Response after the issues/ conflicts have been **unresolved** and have **grown in intensity**.

Score	Style		Score	Style
___	_____		___	_____
___	_____		___	_____
___	_____		___	_____
___	_____		___	_____
___	_____		___	_____
___	_____		___	_____
___	_____		___	_____
___	_____		___	_____
___	_____		___	_____
___	_____		___	_____
___	_____		___	_____

Potential challenges for you

Directing: assertive & uncooperative – own goals at other's expense. High on product, low on people.

Accommodating: unassertive & cooperative – neglecting one's own concerns to satisfy the other. High on people, low on product.

Avoiding: unassertive & uncooperative – neglecting both one's own and the other's concerns by not addressing the issue. Low on people and product.

Collaborating: assertive & cooperative – digging into an issue to satisfy both parties completely. High on people and product.

Compromising: intermediate in both assertiveness and cooperation – attempting to satisfy partially both oneself and the other by finding a middle ground. Middling on people and product.

With an X for each, mark your preferred styles (calm and storm) on the graph.

Directing   Collaborating

Compromising

TASK

Avoiding   Accommodating

PEOPLE

Think of an example of your style in a recent conflict.

Understanding yourself and working with different conflict styles

Understanding your own conflict style will help you to love, live, and work with people whose styles are different from your own. Read and discuss the suggestions for your conflict styles with people who live or work with you. Do they agree or disagree with what is suggested? Perhaps they will read through the descriptions and recognize their own styles. Communicating about your styles enables you to bring out the best in each other! As you get familiar with the styles, you will find yourself detecting styles even in other people. You will have an idea about how to respond in situations that previously confounded you.

How to bring out the best in someone who scores high in *directing*

- People who use the *directing* style are often task-oriented. They are usually highly productive and concerned to get the job done. Engage them and let them know you are committed to the task at hand or to resolving the issue satisfactorily. If you need time to think things through or cool down, they are usually fine if you ask for this, as long as you indicate clearly a commitment to returning to resolve things. You will get a more positive response if you state specifically when you will come back (for example, in an hour or tomorrow at nine o'clock).

- Although their task focus makes it easy to forget the feelings and needs of others, many *directors* feel deeply responsible for those around them and may feel quite bad if they realize they have wounded them. Look for ways to engage them about the needs of others in settings where they are not in the middle of a big job.

- *Directors* usually prefer to deal with things now and get anxious when others are silent or passive. Don't withdraw without giving some clue about where you stand. Lack of information will increase their anxiety or anger.

- A *directing* person who is angry can be very intimidating, for this style is the most active and "in your face" when anger is high. If this person has a history of abusing others emotionally or otherwise and holds more power than you, look for a path to safety or shelter. If the person is basically healthy emotionally, simply asking for a chance to cool off and think often helps, as long as you state clearly your intention to return and work on things.

How to bring out the best in someone who scores high in *collaborating*

- People who use *collaborating* a lot function best when you are direct and clear with them about what you need. They have their opinions and needs, of course, and their preference for *collaborating* gives them a desire to state them. But they really do want to hear from you as well. If you are put off by their tendency to be direct, particularly if you quickly back off and don't say what you want, they are likely to get frustrated and anxious. Too much accommodating on your part makes them feel as if they are directing, which is not at all their desire.

- Let them know that you really want to hear their concerns.

- Bring a blend of task and relationship focus to the conversation. Move toward them.

- Like the directing style, *collaborators* need information about what is going on from others and get anxious if others pull away without providing information about what is going on. Don't withdraw or move away without giving a clear explanation (for example, "I want to go for a walk for half an hour to think things through, then I'll come back and we can talk some more").

How to bring out the best in someone who scores high in *avoiding*

- *Avoiders* benefit more than any other style from an offer to give them time and/or space to withdraw and think things through. You are more likely to get a "yes" answer about anything you need from them if you use a two-step approach. The first step is to let *avoiders* know – in thoughtful tones – what you want and that you'd like them to think about this. Then come back later – an hour, a day, a week – and hear their response.

- Stay low-key. The more intense or demanding you are, the more likely the *avoider* will go into major withdrawal.

- There is a significant subgroup of conflict *avoiders* who are actually quite task-focused, but in a particular way. They bring a high level of caution and attention to detail to everything they do; they are concerned not to put important things at risk. They are highly focused on data, information, or preserving hard-won resources or traditions. Look for ways to provide them with information – about plans, options, costs, rules, anticipated results or consequences, precedents, dates, etc. Part of what they need is to see that others take seriously the concern to avoid risks, for they see these more clearly than anyone else. By providing them with information, you help them to know that you, too, have your eyes open.

- Haste in decision-making tends to push *avoiders* into withdrawal or analysis paralysis. Move slowly, one step at a time.

How to bring out the best in someone who scores high in *compromising*

- *Compromisers* have a strong sense of reciprocity. More than other styles, they are likely to respond in kind if you back off somewhat from your original position. Leave room negotiate when you make your opening request.

- *Compromisers* value fairness and moderation. Think and speak in terms of "being fair", "fair play", "reasonable", "you give some, I give some", "give and take", etc.

- *Compromisers* tend to value efficiency of time and energy, and are eager to find a way through to a practical solution that ends the difficulty. A sense that a fair and moderate deal was achieved probably matters more than talking through all options.

- As the *compromiser* does not enjoy prolonged debate, a determined conflict partner in *directing* style may, with strong logic, be able to persuade a *compromiser* that they are wrong, creating an appearance that the more forceful person has "won". However, the victory may be hollow. The *compromiser's* deep inner sense that conclusions should be reciprocal and balanced will be disturbed. Trust, openness, and cooperativeness will suffer in the long term. Find concessions for the *compromiser*, even if you are sure your argument is stronger.

How to bring out the best in someone who scores high in *accommodating*

- *Accommodators* want to please and be pleased. Pay attention to small social niceties. More than any other style, *accommodators* will be positively affected by gestures of thoughtfulness – a kind note, an appreciative comment, flowers, a chocolate bar, a card, for example.

- You will get more cooperativeness in doing serious work with *accommodators* if you use a two-step approach. First, connect with them at a human level (ask how they are doing, inquire about a family member, tease a little, thank them for something). Then, and only then, settle down to business. The human connection always comes before work for *accommodators* (an insight that is especially difficult for task-oriented *directors* to remember).

- Stay light. Seriousness or heaviness in others quickly stirs anxiety in *accommodators* and makes it hard for them to focus or stay on task. Use humour. Appreciate the relationship or their good qualities out loud if you can honestly do so.

- Assure *accommodators* repeatedly that you really want to know their preferences and views. Thank them sincerely if they do level with you. If they bring criticism, thank them generously – it requires great effort for *accommodators* to be direct about anything negative.

- In meetings or extended conversations with *accommodators*, take breaks and lighten up on a regular basis. Long, heavy discussion unsettles *accommodators* and pushes them to unhelpful places more quickly than other styles.

The self-discovery quizzes help us with the first steps of IC, "Branching": understanding our perspective and the perspective of our conflict partner. We offer another tool to increase self-and others-understanding.

Acknowledgment

Kraybill, R., "Style Matters: The Kraybill Conflict Style Inventory", is copyrighted material included here under special license of the publisher, Riverhouse ePress, and can be reproduced only by permission of the publisher. For licensing information, see the copyright page of this book.

What's inside? The Big 5 personality traits[6]
Another powerful framework for understanding personality differences that has stood the test of very large-scale meta-analyses is called the Big 5. Five big personality factors have emerged from the meta-analyses of hundreds of studies, and these account for a large amount of personality variety among people. Each of us is somewhere on these Big 5 dimensions:

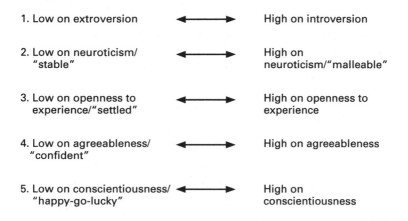

1. Low on extroversion ⟵⟶ High on introversion

2. Low on neuroticism/ ⟵⟶ High on
   "stable" neuroticism/"malleable"

3. Low on openness to ⟵⟶ High on openness to
   experience/"settled" experience

4. Low on agreeableness/ ⟵⟶ High on agreeableness
   "confident"

5. Low on conscientiousness/ ⟵⟶ High on
   "happy-go-lucky" conscientiousness

(Note: Being high on one dimension does not necessarily mean we are high on other dimensions. The dimensions are independent of each other; for example, we can be high on extroversion, and low on agreeableness, or vice versa.)

These categories can be misused to put others in a box or to justify one's inflexibility. "I'm an introvert and it's lights out every night at nine o'clock come hell or high water. That's what works for me." Or "You're high on agreeableness and openness to experience, remember? You won't mind fifty guests for Sunday lunch in about an hour! You love that sort of thing; it's who you are." Yes, we can misuse personality categories, but as tools for reflection to increase self-awareness they're really useful. Our score is not as important as recognizing our tendencies. We all fall somewhere along each spectrum. As noted with the self-discovery quizzes, differences and similarities can lead to clashes, so it's a good idea to think about our preferences and to be alert to others' tendencies and preferences.

We can think about these personality traits as if they are items we possess, such as a Rolex watch or a Gucci bag. "I have extroversion, and you have introversion." Another way of thinking about personality is to apply the IC lens.

1. Extrovert v. introvert

Outgoing **extroverts** are hungry for more stimulation and interaction, and get energy by being with other people. Therefore, we can think of outgoing extroverts as people who direct their perception – their lens – to the real world out there, to people, to where the action is. Extroverts enjoy lots of relationships; if there is a party, the extrovert is there!

Introverts, who are less outgoing than extroverts, have their lens attuned to their inner world within. People who score high on introversion find their own thoughts, perceptions, and feelings so vital and interesting that hardly any further stimulation is needed. No less loving and kind than extroverts, however, introverts are somewhat exhausted by those noisy people in the outside world.

2. Malleable v. stable

We're calling people who score high on the neuroticism scale **malleable** because "neurotic" is often used colloquially as an insult. These people are normal people who have a more malleable nervous system that responds quickly and powerfully to potential threat. Slam the door and those high on neuroticism will jump out of their seats. Their lens is attuned to potential dangers, whether an on-rushing car or an angry boss. They tend to focus on the negatives and on potential problems, within themselves as well as the world out there.

People who score low on neuroticism, also called "**stable**", have a central nervous that is not so reactive. Their lens on danger is not so focused. They are cool customers and are not as unsettled by potential threat. They are still in their seats when you slam that door. Humans have evolved to protect themselves from danger; "stables" do this in an unruffled way. They will not be focusing primarily on threat, negatives, or problems, even when that is called for.

3. Openness to experience v. settled

People who score high on **openness to experience** have a big lens on life, a lens that wants more of life's experience and is eager for more information. They are ready to ditch the old understanding. Their lens is like a huge astronomical lens focused on the farthest reaches, hungry for more, even if it contradicts what they already believe. People who score low on openness to experience, or what we call "**settled**", are saying in effect, "What I can see in my lens is enough. It all makes sense; I like it. I don't want to upset it." Whatever size their lens on life, they aren't looking for more. They are settled and are happy with what they see.

4. Agreeableness v. confident

People who score high on **agreeableness** have a lens that

focuses on warm relationship with other people. Intimacy is desired, and therefore other people's approval and other people's emotional comfort is important. Their lens weaves together the perspective of self and others, aiming for closeness and harmony between them. If necessary, they will focus on what others want, not what they want. People who score low on agreeableness, or what we call "**confident**", are less focused on how others feel. They don't need their perspective to match the perspective of others. It doesn't matter what others think! Unburdened by a need for agreement with the perspectives of others, they can show their disagreement with gusto and get on with their own interests.

5. *Conscientious v. happy-go-lucky*
People who score high on **conscientiousness** have a sharply focused lens on the details and duties that they should fulfil. Their eye is on the clock; they are not late for their appointments and keep in mind the expectations of the other. Their focus is never blurred; having read the fine print, they can tick all the boxes, knowing what their duty is.
People who score low on conscientiousness, or what we call "**happy-go-lucky**", have a blurry lens on the details and duties towards others. Free of the fine print, their focus is not close up on the details and duties of social interaction. They may not RSVP or fill in all the blanks on the form. They just don't notice these things.

Inevitably, a basic level of conflict with other people arises from these normal personality differences: "You are always wanting loads of friends over, but I want some peace and quiet"; "Oh, you are looking at the big picture, whereas I am really concerned about this one tiny but crucial detail"; "You never phone back, but I can't sleep until I've replied to all my messages." Conflict between people is heightened if we think these differences are personal slights. In reality, these personality differences amount to the different kind of focus we have on self, other, and the world. Our ways of perceiving – our lenses – are different.

Just to make things a little more complicated, we can also conflict with those who are similar to us. Two "confidents" might really annoy one another, each thinking the other is not very considerate. Or two "malleables" might get on each other's nerves, wishing the other would just calm down and not be so jumpy. We often recognize in others what we cannot see in ourselves. At least some of the irritation comes from looking in a mirror; on some level we recognize ourselves and it is too painful so we just focus on the other person. This happens in close relationships. We often turn on the other person when we're really upset with ourselves. If we ever find ourselves very angry with our partner, family member, friend, or colleague, then we can take a moment to consider whether we're actually mad at ourselves about something. Maybe we didn't handle something in the way we wanted to, so we focus on the failings of someone else, unconsciously, to make ourselves feel better.

Wherever we land on each Big 5 spectrum, there is no better or worse. Each tendency brings its own pros and cons. On some level, we recognize this. We may wish to have a conscientious secretary (who RSVPs) but prefer to go on holiday with our happy-go-lucky, unconscientious best friend. Differences are normal. *Vive la différence!*

Whatever our Big 5 profile, conflict style, and way of

seeing the world, we have as good a chance at transforming conflict as anyone else. The ability to *transform* conflict (defined as being able to ascend the seven IC levels through branching and weaving, seeing different perspectives and weaving them together in win–win ways) is determined not by personality traits, responses to disagreement, or different ways of seeing the world. The ability to transform conflict depends on a person's level of self-awareness. To branch and weave, we need to be able to have some critical distance from ourselves. We need to see the man or woman in the mirror, not through overly critical lenses ("Oh, I'm no good at all in anything") and not through overly inflated lenses ("Oh, yes, I'm good in all things at all times"). We need to see ourselves as we are, our preferences, tendencies, strengths, and foibles. We need to acknowledge how we feel and what we think. We need self-honesty. And then, like a good army general, we need to take a step back from ourselves and perceive our perspective on the conflict at hand, our branch, our thoughts and feelings, our vision for the future, as well as all of this for our "opponent". Only through lots of branching, using all the tools, strategies, and skills introduced in this chapter, and through lots of weaving, can we direct any successful operations in the field of conflict. Instead of battle, we're really talking about peacemaking.

• Think about what your Big 5 profile might be. Which snapshot descriptions ring most true for you?
• Link the Big 5 traits you see in yourself with your results from the self-discovery quizzes:
How might your Big 5 traits connect with how you see the world, how you respond to conflict or differences

of opinion, how you blend your concern for the relationship and the task/issue, how you behave when anxious?

• In conflict, what often feels personal to you, but really may be more a matter of interpersonal difference or similarity?

Core to self-discovery is the practice of listening – listening to ourselves and then listening to our partners, family members, friends, and colleagues. All of us have been listening since ears formed on the sides of our heads, but very few of us are good at really hearing what other people are saying. Even a naturally listening ear closes down in the heat of the moment. With the limbic system on red alert, we're all likely to shout...

I already know what you're going to say and I don't like it!

We can't slow ourselves down during those crucial ninety seconds if we're not listening to the signs of panic pulsing through our bodies. Listening to our stress signals enables us to use the slow and prime steps to calm down (deep breathing, taking time out, using a physical cue). Maybe we now feel calmer, but we're struggling to listen to the perspective of our conflict partner. Without listening skills, we slow down and go nowhere.

Most of us think we are good listeners, but unfortunately most of us are pretty poor at it. We get distracted, thinking we know what the other person is going to say. Maybe we're not that interested in the other point of view: our own branch on the conflict tree is so fascinating, why see any other branches or viewpoints? And we have a lot invested in our viewpoint. It matters to us. It may seem as if we're just talking about not being late all the time, but really there's more at stake here: issues of fairness, respect for others, and, come to think of it, our frustration that our friend is dating someone who's no good for them. The initial disagreement is often just the tip of the iceberg, an excuse to vent frustration about other seemingly unrelated tension points. OK, we'll listen for a second, just to reassure ourselves we're right – we're on the best branch – but we quickly return to our viewpoint, tuning out the rest of the scenery. Branching? No need. We're in the best spot. Just need to hang on for dear life.

How did we get here?
We begin by learning to listen to ourselves. Learning how to listen to ourselves (or not) occurs through our interactions with other people, primarily our parents or carers. Technically, it's called "mirroring". Parents do this when they tell the child what they see them doing: "You want to suck your little finger? That tastes good, doesn't it? Oh, now you want to look at your cuddly toy. He's jolly, isn't he? Look at how far you can throw the toy! What a strong little girl you are!" Being seen is a fundamental human need that enables us to see ourselves. This type of interaction is important for brain development.

We might not have been mirrored very well or consistently as children. Perhaps a sibling mirrored us while we were small, but then they went off to school and weren't around any more. Maybe it wasn't culturally or socially acceptable, or our parents were in crisis or busy. It can be difficult to do something for ourselves or others that wasn't consistently shown to us. We may have got enough to develop into

138

competent, functioning adults, but most of us can always do with more self-awareness. We can become our own mirrors. Listening to ourselves, we can learn to notice – be mindful of – our thoughts, feelings, and ideas. Giving ourselves this kind of self-care is terrific. We have some interesting things going on in our heads and hearts.

The problem arises when we do not turn our mirroring process outward, toward the rest the world. Me, myself, and I can be rather absorbing. We might share our scintillating thoughts or keep them to ourselves, but, either way, our focus can stay glued on us. Are people agreeing with us? Do they recognize the value in what we're saying? We don't have the space in our heads for any other points of view. We want them to make room for us.

This struggle is not about arrogance or humility. Even when we think we're as low as pond scum, there is still a preoccupation with ourselves that prevents us from listening to others. Other people might praise us, point out our strengths, but, no, we dismiss their praise. We know the truth. We may have heard it from our parents or carers, our teachers, or so-called friends. We are no good. We "de-compliment" without even noticing that we've just trashed another person's viewpoint that praised us.

Whether we think we're fabulous, rubbish, or somewhere in between, most of us struggle to hear others' points of view until we learn active listening skills.

Active listening: Three small steps for us…
three giant leaps for humankind
Walking is part of what it means to be human. Walking on the moon – well, that's something else. Only a few people can do that. Similarly, active listening involves one of the most

basic physiological processes common to living creatures, but listening to other people while in the midst of conflict is different. The good news is that anyone can do it and the impact is just as extraordinary. Your three small steps[7] can turn around an entire situation, lowering the tension, diffusing the anger and bad feelings, and moving the situation into a place of learning. It can represent three giant leaps forward for your relationship, your group, and your whole community.

1. Mirror: We begin by reflecting back to the speaker what we heard them say: "So what I hear you saying is…" We try to capture the essence, rather than parroting. Sometimes we use their words; sometimes we summarize in our own words. Our tone and posture show that we are interested, engaged, and focused on the speaker. We make and keep eye contact, giving them space but remaining physically near. If the speaker goes on at length, then we respectfully interrupt, saying we'll mirror back what they've said so far so that we don't forget anything, and then invite them to continue. If we don't understand something, we ask a clarifying question. We avoid passing judgment or expressing disagreement. Our goal is to understand where they're coming from, to identify what is important to them.

2. Validate: After we've heard the speaker and mirrored it back accurately, we let the speaker know that we see their viewpoint: "OK, that makes sense to me. I get where you're coming from." This does not mean that we agree with them. We probably won't agree with what they've said, but, based on how the speaker sees the situation, we can see how they might think what they think. We resist our limbic urges to defend ourselves or to attack.

3. Empathize: Finally we try to imagine how they must feel. Angry? Sad? Nervous? Stressed? We tentatively tell the speaker what we think they might be feeling: "Ah, you might be feeling somewhat disappointed?" We let the speaker correct us: "Well, sort of, but I think my stronger feeling is just sadness." "Ah, you feel sad... and perhaps hopeless?" "Yeah. Maybe." We explore their feelings from inside their point of view. Having already explored our own perspective, values, and feelings, we can keep our reactive limbic system on a lower gear. We are showing this person great love – because they're another human being or because we're deeply committed to them – by giving them the space to have their own views and feelings. We want to understand them better. Yet we don't acquiesce to their viewpoint or lose our own stance. We are branching so that we can do some weaving.

Throughout active listening we can use the slow and prime steps to keep ourselves calm and able to hear the speaker (deep breathing, taking time out, visual numbers).

Sadly, the steps of active listening can be misused to manipulate people into feeling safe so that they do what we want them to do. Most of us are so starved for a listening ear that when we find one we can be lulled into doing something we don't want to do. Similarly, we know how to listen to someone so they feel understood and then we steer them into doing our bidding, withholding our listening and understanding when they begin to object. If we avoid misusing active listening, then it will retain its transforming power.

Upsetting the apple cart: Listening spreads around the power
Listening humanizes our opponent and our opponent. But
our opponent is never as human as we are (or else they'd
agree with us!). For this reason, the act of listening is one of
the most subversive acts we can perform: it empowers both
the speaker and the listener.

The word "subversive" can both frighten and excite. But
whatever we are doing in our conflict now, it is not working
or we would not be looking for help. So something that
subverts the status quo – the current situation – can only be
good. We want something to shift, to get unstuck, and it will
take something subversive to disrupt the deadlock. Listening
detonates power. It explodes the myth that power is a limited
pie. We don't lose our share of the power pie if someone
else gets a slice. Power in conflict is an organic dynamic that
multiplies as more people share it.

Active listening skills are notoriously difficult to hone.
We all fall back into defending, judging, and "fixing".
Don't despair. Practice really does help.

1. Enlist a couple of friends. Designate one of you
a speaker, one a listener, and one an observer. The
observer keeps time. The speaker talks about something.
The listener practises mirroring, validating, and
empathizing. The observer calls time (ten to fifteen
minutes) and gives feedback on how the listener did.
Then switch roles until everyone has played each role
once.
2. Practise on the hoof, incognito as it were –
• as a friend talks while walking or driving

- over dinner while friends or family members talk about their day
- on the telephone, as a colleague vents their frustration with a client during a committee meeting
- at a meeting while a fellow volunteer states their views
- other situations?

At this point in the process of conflict transformation, it can be helpful to take stock of what we've learned. We've been taking steps to slow and prime. We've reviewed and acted on what we've learned through the self-discovery quizzes, and Big 5 lenses. We've deployed active listening skills. It may be that through our use of these tools, our branching has led to weaving. We've identified a creative way forward that integrates our concerns and the concerns of our conflict partner into a win–win solution. It may be, however, that we don't know how to move forward. Reflecting on the level of conflict we're in can help.

Conflict levels: The cork is going to blow... and it's not champagne
After we assess the tension in a conflict, we can act to lower it.[8]

Conflict level 1: Goal is to learn and grow
During this level, we slow and prime, act on the insights from the quizzes and Big 5 lenses, deploy our active listening skills, and start weaving. We're kind of enjoying this!

Alas, most of our relationship conflicts do not even touch down at this level. They climb straight up. The wall of biological and social obstacles to conflict transformation is forbidding and looming taller with every passing minute.

Conflict level 2: Goal is self-protection
At this level, we feel threatened and defensive. Freeze, flee, or fight are in action. We're trying to protect ourselves from feelings of hurt and disappointment. Our world view is under threat, we're feeling let down, and we're on the attack. Our conflict partner is trying to protect themselves from our attack, defending themselves and then fleeing. Or we might be on the receiving end of an attack, trying to defend ourselves and hide.

We need to slow and prime, reminding ourselves about what we value in the relationship, what is most important to us. Drawing on the self-discovery quizzes and Big 5 lenses, we start to recognize the dynamics in this relationship, how our differences and/or similarities play out in conflict. Trust can build as we identify interpersonal differences and realize the disagreement is not personal. Taking some time for solitude, we reflect on our perspective and what we know about the viewpoint of our conflict partner. We take a risk and initiate a discussion. We ask them to tell us what is going on and stick to the three small steps. Deploying our active listening skills, some genuine communication can start to replace attack and counter-attack. Using the slow and prime steps, we engage non-defensively and keep the bigger picture in mind. With all of this branching (listening to the other's viewpoint), the tension lowers to level 1, where weaving becomes possible.

Conflict level 3: Goal is to win
At this level, our world view is under attack and that's not allowed. We are correct, they are wrong, and we *will* win. Our conflict partner has the same attitude and we are locked in battle. We are going to show the other person that our way is the only way. Our conflict partner is intent on the same goal.

We're in a deadlock.

This conflict level is make or break: up is bleak, down is hopeful. Use slow and prime to calm down. Pay attention to distorted thinking: universalized thinking that moves one situation into "always" or "never" ("You never call me!" "You always hurt my feelings!") coupled with magical knowledge about what the other person is thinking ("I know what you're thinking. You're thinking about how to get back at me because I'm not going to cover for you with the boss again." Really the other person was thinking about what to eat for lunch). These ways of thinking take us down the road to disaster. When we hear ourselves or our conflict partner speak using universalized or magical thinking, we can slow and prime again and again. Reflect on the conflict. What are the interpersonal differences at work? Sketching or jotting down our thoughts and feelings will bring some clarity. What do we think our conflict partner needs to be able to engage constructively? Only when we feel ourselves out of limbic panic should we approach the other person, asking them to tell us their perspective and using active listening skills to hear what they say. If we know that direct communication threatens our conflict partner, then we can use humour or a story to help them to relax and trust us again. If we know they need to feel reassured about the relationship, then we can tell them how important it is to us.

Conflict level 4: Goal is to hurt or get rid of other person
At this level, we start to lay traps for our conflict partner, to prove that we are right. Our conflict partner does the same and it becomes a game of cat and mouse. We are taking emotional, mental, and possibly even physical shots at one another (responding to any protests with disingenuous

excuses such as "Can't you take a joke?" or "I'm just being playful. Relax!"). The scene is not pretty.

With the tension up to this level, we need to impose strict rules on any interaction – time limits, certain topics off-limits, certain behaviours and words (insults, sarcasm, hostile looks) leading to the immediate ending of the meeting – to prevent further harm. "Help" is the key word. Look for a mediator to help to find a mutually satisfactory way forward. Ask for help with communication so that trust can be rebuilt. Patience will help a lot. Seek and accept help from skilled people. Take it slowly.

Conflict level 5: Goal is to destroy the other person
At this stage, we are fighting not just dirty but mean and nasty.

Tension cannot get any higher and it is important to cut off all interaction without a third party present and to find an arbitrator, someone who will make a decision about the conflict that both parties commit to abide by.

The scenarios of levels 4 and 5 may seem far away from the realm of possibilities in our lives, but they indicate a trajectory for conflict if it is not seized as a gift, as a learning opportunity. The fall-out can be ruined lives and strained communities. Not usually acknowledged outside the offices of solicitors, GPs, social workers, and counsellors is the fact that well-resourced people holding responsible jobs and living in peaceful communities find themselves doing things they never imagined themselves doing because the tension level in a disagreement went unchecked, grew, and then exploded.

If we catch ourselves thinking about, imagining, or wanting to hurt our partner, friend, or colleague, then we can take a deep breath and tell someone who can help us work through our thoughts and feelings without harming ourselves or another person.

Think of a present or recent conflict. Assess the conflict level. What can you do or could you have done to lower the tension? What would you do now if you found yourself in the same situation?

Now that we've gone through the tools, strategies, and skills, we need to assemble everything into a peacemaking armoury that will take us up the seven levels of IC.

The A to Z of IC: Getting from 1 to 7
Remember the IC continuum:

Level 1	Level 3	Level 5	Level 7
One point of	Several points of view,	Several points of view,	Many points of view,
	no integration	some integration	integrated into a win–win solution
No branching	Branching	Branching	Much branching
No weaving	No weaving	*Some* weaving	Much weaving

Each of us has a baseline IC level and for most of us it is pretty low, around 1 or 2 out of 7. At level 1, we see only one viewpoint. As our IC rises up to level 7, we see more viewpoints and connections among the viewpoints until we have a broad understanding of the conflict, the context, the people involved, and the contribution of many factors to the conflict (for example, interpersonal differences, past developmental and formational experiences, current commitments and responsibilities).

IC step 1: Branching
1a. We begin by examining our own branch, our perspective on the conflict.

Using the steps of slow and prime (deep breathing, taking time out, using visual clues), we get through the first ninety seconds of conflict reaction so we can reflect. We think about our viewpoint. How does it reflect my tendencies and preferences discussed in Chapters 2 and 3? How does it reflect the way I see the world and my responses to conflict and differences of opinion? How does it reflect my personality traits?

What are my thoughts, feelings, values in this conflict? What is the bigger picture? What are my goals?

Write them down, sketch them, or draw a mind-map. If we try to keep everything in our heads, we'll forget. Let's get to know every aspect of our branch.

1b. Next, we examine the other branches, the other perspectives on this conflict.

We ask ourselves what we know about the perspective of the other person(s) in the conflict, their thoughts, feelings, and values. Putting aside just for now that we disagree with them, we try to get inside their viewpoint. This is brainstorming without judging. What do we think is their bigger picture? What are their goals? Using the earlier chapters, self-discovery quizzes, and Big 5 lenses, what might their tendencies and preferences be?

When we feel ready, we arrange a time and place to use our newly honed active listening skills to find out where they're coming from. We might start to feel anxious again, and so we use the slow and prime steps to calm down our limbic system. Our conflict partner might show signs of anxiety, so we try to show that we're trustworthy, picking up on clues as to what their conflict style might be and using the recommended strategies to help them to relax. We use the conflict levels to determine the tension level and what needs to happen to get it down to level 1, just enough tension to generate creativity. We focus on understanding their viewpoint. After we've finished listening, we write down their perspective. We know we won't remember it all without writing it down.

Now we try to imagine other points of view. We might imagine that other people we know are in the same conflict with us. What do we imagine they might think, feel, value? We try to brainstorm as many viewpoints as possible, putting as much on paper as helpful. As we finish this step, we are operating around IC level 3.

If this is a big conflict, then we might need to spend a few days, a week, or even longer just on branching. We can take our time, without losing momentum. We want to move to the next step – weaving – when we are ready.

IC step 2: Weaving
2. We begin by reviewing our notes. Do we see any themes? Do we notice any shared values or desires? Noticing shared underlying themes, values, or desires takes us toward IC level 5. Making as many connections as possible among the different perspectives, we try to identify the context and type or category of the conflict. Coloured pens or pencils can help us to code our notes, a different colour for each major theme, each context, each category.

Some themes are really sub-themes of broader themes. How might we address opposing perspectives on that theme? How might we weave together several themes? Is there one most important, overarching theme? What's the underlying conflict or tension? What is a creative way forward that addresses the concerns expressed by the underlying tension?

This last step is both exciting and frustrating. We try one solution, then another. We take a break and do something else. We might need a day, a week, a month, or longer to get to a win–win solution that satisfies both parties. This means we hang on to our own viewpoint and our own deepest values, even while we seek to weave a win–win solution with our conflict partner.

How to weave win–win solutions
Are there any strategies that will leverage us to a level 7 insight? Here are two examples:

1) Make a figure–ground reversal

As we branch and weave our way up the IC levels, what we thought was the focus of the conflict moves to the background and what we thought was just background noise moves to centre stage (becoming the focus or central "figure"). Perhaps the initial focus in our conflict was that our flatmate didn't take out the recycling after they said they would. For our flatmate, perhaps the initial focus was not being hassled about something they consider unimportant. As each takes on board the other's perspective, they experience a figure–ground reversal. The initial focus of the conflict – our flatmate not taking out the recycling and us hassling our flatmate – moves to the background. Questions about how we can cooperate while living in the same flat, sharing household management tasks, caring for the environment, going through the ups and downs of work and dating relationships, and being trustworthy, move to the foreground. What seemed like background noise, peripheral to the conflict, becomes the central figure. The higher we move up the IC levels, the more our focus flips back and forth until there is an integration of both the figure and the ground.

2) Focus on unlikely partnerships

At first glance, different parts of the conflict will seem to be completely unrelated. At eighth and ninth glance, we start to see connections between these seemingly unrelated parts. As you integrate, or weave together, these disparate parts into an overarching understanding of the conflict, you discover a way forward.

Here is a scenario showing many factors woven together into a level 7 solution:

Rosie and Troy are in conflict about household management. Both want to be on the same team and want to help one another, but they interpret forgetting differently.

Each wants to be connected and separate in different ways. For Rosie, being part of the same team involves follow-through. Forgetting is bad and you make up for it right away. For Troy, being part of the same team involves reminders without deadlines. Forgetting is no big deal and you deal with it when you can.

Rosie and Troy want to stay in relationship and to grow together. They learn that they bring to the relationship different family histories about levels of concern and aptitudes for household management tasks. Rosie grew up with each family member pitching in and learning to do whatever is needed. Troy grew up with one person taking primary responsibility and the others not thinking much about it. Each of them is affected by what is going on at work, but in opposite ways. If work is going well, household stuff is no big deal for Troy: he pitches in. But if work is frustrating, then household stuff is a chore he'll put off and forget. For Rosie, if work is frustrating, then household stuff becomes all-important. But if work is going well, then she lets household stuff slide. Each of them can fall down on the job in different ways, depending on how what they learned growing up interacts with how their work is going. The disagreement feels personal – "You don't help out!" "You won't stop nagging me!" – but there are complicated interpersonal differences and anxiety responses playing out in the conflict.

Rosie and Troy decide to set a weekly time frame for household management tasks. Each person can do their tasks whenever they want as long as it happens during that week. Reminders are put on a board, not spoken. Each person is in charge of the tasks that they think are most important. If Rosie forgets and starts to hassle Troy, or if Troy forgets and doesn't do his tasks, then whoever forgets has to do a task for the other one. Each commits to telling the other how things are going at work and this helps them to support one another and to adjust expectations about what is going to happen at home.

With this scenario we get some sense of how much slowing and priming, self-discovery, active listening, and movement down the conflict levels is involved in conflict transformation. But the pay-off is the personal growth and relational growth that results. We move to a new level of being and relating.

What about when we are people who aren't self-aware, who don't want to be self-aware, who think it's nonsense? How do we transform conflict if our loved one has those attitudes? Well, we're in a tough spot. But not all is lost. There are ways to transform the conflict, because if we change, then the conflict will change. And sometimes when we change, the other person starts to look in the mirror. The next chapter focuses on the difficult people who like to blame everyone else and not take any responsibility themselves. Of course, that might be us, but every once in a while it really isn't. We really do love, live, and work with someone who is… well, difficult. The good news is that we can experience transformation through conflict even with very difficult people.

CHAPTER 5

You made me do it

It's always the other person's fault. "You make me so angry... You are so stubborn... You did this on purpose... You always want your own way... You never listen to me."

Our primitive limbic system encourages us to view our conflict partner in this way: simplified, with only the bad parts highlighted. All the good parts are ignored. They are to blame. We see ourselves as the innocent victim in the conflict.[1] We are simply defending truth, sanity, righteousness... and our right to exist.

But we are getting beyond this now. We have learned to slow and prime. We have practiced active listening. We are doing the work of IC. We branch out from our closed-down point of view, our "centre of the universe" position. We become able to perceive that, despite our differences, there is something valid in how the other person views the situation. We understand their deeper values, what is really important to them. We are aiming for high IC, weaving their deep values with our own.

Then we hit a brick wall. Our conflict partner takes advantage of our olive branch. They do not perceive our point of view. They are thinking in black and white, and they are "right". Their persistent low IC reignites our low IC, and we are back to where we started: "You make me so angry... You are so stubborn... You never listen to me." And so on.

We may be tempted to give up hope at this point, having tried so hard. In most situations, the high-IC approach to transforming conflict is amazingly powerful. But there are some conflict partners who will require a modified approach. This chapter helps us to identify difficult conflict partners. It teaches us how to engage with people who lack, for whatever reason, the self-insight that enables high IC.

Both parties need to raise IC in order to reach the desired win–win outcome, and not all people can do that. No matter how hard *we* try, we can't raise the IC for other people. In fact, others can drag us down to their level of IC. Research shows that people tend to match the IC level of the other.[2] If your loved one or colleague deals with conflict at a very low level of IC, you are likely to lower your IC level to match theirs. Conflict with a difficult person is likely to get worse, not better, without tailored approaches.

Some rare people are unilaterally high in IC all the time but may be taken advantage of by those who can't or won't see their viewpoint. It is only when both parties engage in high IC levels that we find our way to win–win collaborative solutions. It takes two to add up to high IC. So, even when we have calmed our limbic system, moved out of code red, gone beyond our tendency to dehumanize and blame our conflict partner, and actively listened to their point of view, they might not reciprocate. Ever. When this is our experience, it is important not to overlook the warning signs. We may be engaging with a "difficult person".

Jack, aged thirty-eight, comes to the door of the church office with his young bride-to-be. He rings the doorbell – hard – several times. The door is opened, and Jack demands,

"Where is the vicar? I have an appointment." The secretary, embarrassed, apologizes, "I'm so sorry, he isn't here." Finding out the time of the pre-wedding appointment, she happily points out that Jack and his betrothed are some ten minutes early; they are welcome to wait. "But I made an appointment," says Jack, still clearly annoyed.

Alice, the bride-to-be, only notices how much the appointment matters, how much Jack wants to marry her. But perhaps Alice should start to pay attention to whether or not Jack regularly focuses *only* upon his own perspective. If this pattern continues, Alice faces a life of trying to make everything run according to this man's expectations. From this tiny bit of data, it seems that Jack hasn't even arrived at step 1 of IC, branching – that is, understanding that other people inevitably have thoughts and experiences that are different from his. Alice needs to keep an eye on the unfolding pattern of Jack's lens on other people. Noticing recurring patterns of branching and weaving (or lack thereof) will give Alice some clues about what to expect in a conflict with Jack. She will need to plan in advance how to help him take on board her perspective when their first fight erupts.

Questions to ask yourself when preparing to transform conflict

IC step 1: Branching
   • Does my conflict partner (at least sometimes) perceive other people's viewpoints?
   • Are these different viewpoints accorded some validity, even when they disagree?
   • Does my conflict partner hang on to his or her own viewpoint in the face of difference or opposition? Or do they rush to agree?

IC step 2: Weaving
• Does my conflict partner (at least sometimes) weave his or her own and others' viewpoints into some kind of greater weaving, enabling win–win solutions of some kind?

By asking these questions, we attune ourselves to look for signs to help us tailor our own high-IC approach to a level that is realistic vis-à-vis the other person. We look for signs that our conflict partner is in touch with their own viewpoint. Some people are so eager to agree with others that, in practice, they have no stance of their own. We look for signs that this person is able to perceive differing viewpoints. Or can they only see their own? Is this person able to weave different, opposing viewpoints in creative ways that are win–win? We agree that all this is a tall order, something that usually needs to be learned. But if there are no signs of any of these skills in evidence in our conflict partner, then we need to tailor our own approach.

It is probably safe to say that readers who have stayed with us so far are on the road to being able to perceive their own and others' perspectives. Otherwise, this book would have made no sense. Yet, no matter how advanced *we ourselves* are in conflict transformation skills, conflict is going to be really tough going if our conflict partners are unable to take a step back and observe themselves. We may practise all the skills in this book, which work so powerfully in so many contexts, only to find ourselves frustrated in our attempt to resolve conflict with that one really difficult person in our lives. Where do we go from here?

Hyper-advanced IC training: People who really are difficult – not just different from you
Here comes the really advanced training for conflict

transformation. As budding practitioners of high IC, as described in Chapters 2, 3, and 4, our first move in any conflict is always a high-IC move: we calm our own limbic system, get a sense of our own viewpoint, and actively listen to the other's perspective, mirroring it back so that they are assured that we understand what is vital to them. Most people will respond positively to this, and a win–win way to transform the conflict will be found. But what if our conflict partner consistently responds with low IC, taking advantage of our generosity?

Here's the rub. Some people are so glued (fused) to themselves that they cannot get enough critical distance on themselves. They cannot *see* themselves, especially when in conflict. They just react. The limbic system dominates. They lack the self-awareness – a neutral, detached ability to observe themselves – that is crucial for high-IC conflict transformation. They will have difficulty in branching. Weaving will be nearly impossible. Yet they put up powerful barriers to admitting their need for help. They lack the self-awareness even to realize their need. They cannot see themselves. And they do everything possible to avoid seeing themselves.

This does not mean that they are not worthy and valuable people. We may want to stay in this relationship for any number of good reasons. The aim here is not to categorize and condemn other people but to enable us to have realistic expectations and to approach conflict with difficult people without setting ourselves up to fail.

What to expect in conflict with difficult people
There are many forms of psychological suffering that afflict human beings. One broad category pertains to personality disorders (PDs for short). Each separate personality disorder is quite rare in the general population. But, if added together,

most medium-size to large groups – extended families, voluntary organizations, faith communities – have a good chance of having at least one difficult person in their midst. Although people with PDs may be few in number, their impact on others is huge.

People suffering from PDs have often suffered a traumatic or confused upbringing. Their lifestyle as a teenager or adult may have made matters worse, but they are not to be blamed for the early roots of their disorder. They may have addictions or compulsive behaviour – gambling, incessant cleaning of the house. Somehow the development of their personality has become locked into inflexible ways of relating. Although they may be loveable, well-meaning people, their close relationships are a string of disasters, or at least problematic. Work relationships suffer too. They move from job to job. Or they become unemployable, even though they may be talented and intelligent. This difficult person is in touch with reality. They are not mentally ill. They don't hear voices or think their brain is inhabited by aliens. Yet everyone around them suffers from the difficult aspects of this person's personality, despite all the love we feel for them. The difficult person does not feel they have a problem, but certainly other people think they do. Have you ever tried to resolve a conflict with someone who doesn't think they have contributed to the conflict in any way whatsoever? It is extremely hard. From the point of view of the difficult person, the problem is not theirs – the problem is you!

If this sounds like someone you know, the key criteria are the extreme expression of these characteristics, a lack of self-awareness, and no desire to change. Unlike people struggling with depression or anxieties who are miserable in their problem and want help, people with PDs often do not perceive that they have a problem.

*Who, **moi?***

We all have the characteristics of PDs to some extent, but people struggling with PDs have these characteristics to an extreme degree. We should not jump to labelling anyone. PDs are not well understood, and there is much overlap between categories, so we approach the following thumbnail descriptions with humility, knowing that these sketches grossly simplify. For the sake of economy, these sketches omit the background histories and focus on describing the lenses on self and other. These lenses on self and others are crucial for conflict transformation, and so it makes sense to pay attention to these, so that we can tailor our high-IC approach to conflict with difficult people in realistic ways.[3]

Lenses that are out of focus

For people struggling with personality disorders, the lens on oneself and the lens on others are out of focus. Their early years have probably been full of emotional pain or upheaval.[4] Perhaps the lens on the self was distorted by a harsh, critical, bossy parent who continually humiliated their child. The child may have made the choice to rubbish themselves and agree with this demeaning valuation of themselves in order to maintain a secure base with the parent.[5] Now a young adult, they can only see themselves through this negative lens.

For another person, perhaps the lens on others became distorted due to early experiences of being attacked or bullied. These experiences have crystallized into a lens focused on always viewing other people as a threat.

There are recurring distortions in their perceptions of and interactions with others. We all have some of these distortions ourselves, so if we pay attention to our difficult conflict partner's lenses, we can use our empathy to understand what is going on in conflict with them.

Understanding distorted lenses on self and other:
Thumbnail sketches[6]
While reading these sketches you will see something of your self more in some sketches than in others. No need to be overly alarmed. We all have some of these tendencies. The distinction for people with PDs is the *extreme* expression of these tendenices.

The magnified self
(Referred to as *narcissistic personality* in clinical practice)
The lens on the *self* is a magnifying glass. The ego is hugely inflated. They *need* to see the self as special – with special gifts, requiring special treatment. The self is the centre and needs continual adulation and attention.[7] In any conflict, it is the person's own viewpoint that matters. They will not be good at branching; their lens on other people's viewpoints is more like a telescope. Others' viewpoints are seen from far, far away. Other people, and how they view things, aren't very real; they are not 3-D. What counts is the magnified self: this fills the horizon. There will be little attempt to weave together differing viewpoints, as other people are barely perceived. Conflict means "Of course I win".

The magnified other
(Referred to as a *dependent personality*)
The lens on *others* is a magnifying glass. It is *other* people that the dependent person desperately needs. Other people provide a centre for security and self-worth. Relationship with them must be protected at all costs.[8] The lens on self is almost a blank. They feel as if they hardly exist, that they have no centre. They need to revolve around others, for others to tell them what to do. What counts is the magnified other who gives a sense of security and identity. In conflict, there will be little attempt to weave differing viewpoints. Conflict means "You win, I hardly exist".

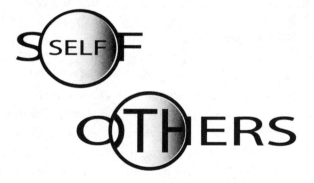

The extreme lens
(referred to as a *borderline personality*)
The lens on **others** is one of extreme contrasts, black or white. It is a lens either of idealization – "You are perfect" – or a lens of devaluation – "You are despicable". This lens is unstable; it can shift. Relationships swing from the extreme of intimacy to a sense of betrayal.[9] The person cannot bear to be alone. They have only a fuzzy sense of self; the lens on self is out of focus. They desperately need to find direction,

identity, or fulfilment. Moods swing; anger flares. Behaviour shifts impulsively. Something is desperately needed, and addictions are one way to fill those needs. In conflict, there will be little ability to branch or weave together opposing viewpoints. Conflict means "Love me or I'll do something extreme".

The theatrical lens
(referred to as a *histrionic personality*)
The lens on self and others is a theatrical lens, a movie camera lens. Others are an audience for a performance of the self. Extravagant emotion is displayed for this lens, but the emotions are actually shallow.[10] The lens on the self is often overly concerned with personal physical attractiveness.

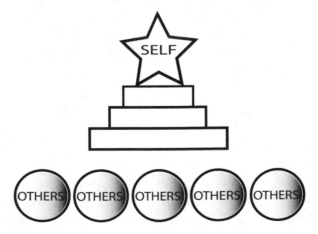

Perhaps conditioned by our celebrity culture, there is a great need to be the centre of attention. Efforts are made to get others' lenses refocused on the self, and, if needed, through seduction. Conflict might be welcomed, not to resolve it but to act out roles of martyrdom or anger. Conflict means "High drama – I am the star of this show!"

The suspicious lens
(Referred to as a *paranoid personality*)
The lens on the self is darkly discoloured. It is suspicious and expects the worst from other people.[11] The lens on others is focused mainly on the negative. The self's badness is thrown outward; it becomes the "badness" of others. It takes a lot of energy to project the bad-self continually on to others, so any criticism or advice is perceived as a huge threat. Suspicious of others, they expect to be hurt. Clashing viewpoints cannot be woven together. Conflict means "I can't afford to be wrong yet again – it has to be all your fault."

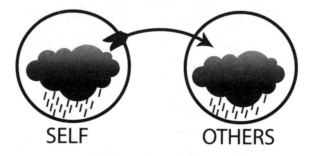

SELF   OTHERS

The detached lens
(referred to as a *schizoid personality*)
The lens on self or other is as distant and detached as possible. The detached person does not enjoy or desire close relationships.[12] The lens is focused purely on the intellectual – or spiritual – aspects of life. Anything to do with the body, emotions, or sex is cut off by the intellect-only lens. Indifferent to praise or closeness, emotions are very repressed. Conflict, if allowed at all, is an intellectual exercise concerning abstract arguments. Conflict means "What conflict?"; real conflict is avoided.

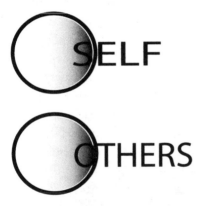

The blank lens
(referred to as a *sociopathic personality*)
The lens on both self and others is blank in parts.[13] The lens on the self and the lens on others have some "head" knowledge, but what is lacking is the ability to feel compassion for others, or even to feel deeply for one's own self. Other people are viewed as a means to get what the self wants. A person who is blank on compassion can figure out other people (and use this cool understanding with charm and cunning), but

there is no empathy for others. Lacking empathy, they lack conscience. If you are in a relationship with someone and begin to feel afraid at a gut level, it may be that you intuit this lack of empathy for you. Get out as soon as you can. Conflict means "I will hurt you".

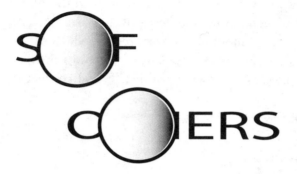

There are also people who can be understood as expressing the characteristics of *avoidant* personalities (who avoid contact with others and are afraid of criticism), *obsessive compulsive* personalities (whose lives are governed by the need for perfection, sometimes expressed in actions such as constant hand washing), *multiple* personality disorders (where the self is fragmented or fractured through trauma), and *schizotypal* personalities (marked by eccentric thoughts and behaviours).[14] As we have said, we all have some of the characteristics of PDs, to some degree. All of us suffer some distortion in how we perceive self and others. But most of us have had enough normal relationship in our lives, enough self-awareness, enough capacity for personal change and growth, so that our eccentric, wounded parts are balanced by some normal functioning. We have been lucky.

Others, less lucky, have suffered extreme distortions in the lens on self and others, as these sketches have portrayed.

There is no blame or shame for these forms of psychological suffering. But we need to be forewarned. A person suffering extreme distortions in their lenses on self and others will find it very difficult, if not impossible, to transform conflict using high IC. They will be *unable* to do some of the following:

Branch
- examine their own perspective
- perceive another's perspective
- treat the other's perspective as valid
- hang on to their own perspective in the face of difference or opposition.

Weave
- integrate their own and another's perspectives into a greater tapestry that brings about a win–win solution of some kind and transforms the conflict.

If we are in a relationship with someone who has some or many of the features in any of the sketches here, we may feel that we can love this person into being able to take on board our perspective. We believe that we can make them feel so loved that they will start to see themselves with more clarity and see others with more understanding. Love conquers all! The evidence from clinical studies suggests otherwise. We need to take a more practical approach.

For this, we modify (but do not abandon) our own high-IC tactics, as in this simplified scenario:

> Our move 1 – Our modified strategy starts out with high IC. We say to our difficult conflict partner, in effect, "I want to understand what you are saying here. I want to understand what is important to you. I am willing to take it on board."
>
> Conflict partner response 1 – Our difficult partner may respond with low IC: "Yeah, well, I told you I was right – do it my way or else.".
>
> Our move 2 – Our next move should meet them where they are at. Our conflict partner has ruled out high-IC collaboration, so we choose another way: "OK, I guess you don't want to understand where I am coming from so we can find a creative way forward [collaborating]. I am not going to impose my wishes on you [directing] and I don't want to have your wishes imposed on me (requiring accommodating on my part). So, the options I can see are that we need to come back to this later [avoiding] or ask someone to help us find a fair way forward (compromising)."

Our difficult conflict partner has met their match. We mirror back where they are at, and provide choices. Also, we have drawn our boundaries so that we are not exploited. We maintain meeting them where they are at for as long as necessary. The key thing is to retain our cool and not react out of the limbic system. The slow and prime steps are vitally important for this process (deep breathing, taking time out, using visual reminders).

With our boundaries demonstrated, we continue using active listening skills. This continues to model that we are willing to listen to their perspective. Our conflict partner may see that stalemate is ahead, unless they return to the higher IC that we are modelling:

Conflict partner response 2 – "Oh, I guess you have a point too..."

Our move 3 – We immediately reward that with, in effect, "Yes, that is exactly what is important to me. I appreciate that you are trying understand what is important to me. And I want to understand what is really important to you in this. Can you tell me what really matters to you here?"

Conflict partner response 3 – "Well, I guess what I really need is..."

And here we see that our conflict partner has risen to our forgiving, rewarding response (our move 3). We are on our way to high-IC solutions.

This sequence of moves follows "Tit for Tat", a computer-based strategy modelling the moves of two opponents. It is a strategy that wins in the end against even the most competitive and aggressive strategies.[15] This sequence is effective because its first move is always generous: "I want to hear what's important to you." It models what high IC looks like. It gives our conflict partner an invitation to respond in kind.

It becomes clear very quickly to our conflict partner what our rules of engagement are. Our conflict partner does not need to rely solely on self-insight (which may be underdeveloped or not possible at this time) but rather is helped to learn IC, at least to some tiny degree, through real-life interaction with a smart, high-IC conflict partner.

So, the Tit for Tat rules are:

- **Generous.** Our first move is always high IC: "I want to hear your perspective."
- **Boundaried.** We will not be exploited beyond one defection. If our conflict partner is not collaborative in response, we mirror back what our conflict partner is doing, present the choices these entail, and draw our boundaries.
- **Forgiving.** If our conflict partner eventually responds collaboratively, we will immediately forgive, taking the conflict discussion back to a place where it's possible to find win–win solutions.

In short, we aim for high-IC collaboration when that is possible. We do not retaliate, no matter how nasty the other person gets. Slow and prime steps are your best friends in resisting urges to retaliate (deep breathing, time out, visual clues. See Chapter 4 for more details). Yet we have boundaries and we present clear choices to the other person. We model high IC flexibly and enable our difficult conflict partner to rise to high IC, if that is possible. We respond positively but not foolishly.

This Tit for Tat flexible strategy enables us to draw on all the conflict approaches, depending upon how the other person responds. For example, we collaborate or compromise if all goes well. We direct if we are in an emergency situation or we have the appropriate authority to be directive. We accommodate if we think this is just about the small stuff. Or, if necessary, we walk away. Avoidance sometimes is our best, or only, choice. High IC involves having as many conflict styles at our fingertips as the context requires, collaborating, avoiding, directing, accommodating, and compromising (see Chapter 4 for a review).

If Tit for Tat fails, six further steps to transform conflict with difficult people

Having tried the Tit for Tat strategy, our conflict remains entrenched. The sad reality may be that our conflict partner may be unable to perceive our perspective, however much we model high IC. This is not a personally aimed affront. It is an *inability*. We would not take personally someone's missing leg or inability to hear. We would accept them as they are. Understanding and accepting a lacking capacity will reduce some of the tension. There is grieving to do here because it is unlikely that this relationship will give us what we had hoped for.

Secondly, it is highly unlikely that by trying harder, *on our own*, we will be able successfully to transform conflict with this person. We need to get professional help. People with PDs require specially tailored and in-depth forms of therapy. New therapies are evolving that are effective in terms of helping people to change their behaviours. There is hope, if the person is willing to get it.[16] Without getting professional help, it is doubtful that we can single-handedly enable this person to transform conflict in a healthy way.

Thirdly, if the difficult person with whom we are in conflict is unwilling to get relationship or personal counselling, we might need to get help for ourselves. In the process, we may discover a few more of our own difficult tendencies and find ways of dealing with them. This will have a positive impact on all our relationships. With the help of counselling for ourselves, we may find ways of making life with this difficult person much more bearable.

Fourthly, we accept that high-IC conflict transformation strategies are unlikely to succeed, even when we have modelled them using Tit for Tat. Our conflict partner lacks the self-insight to enable them to learn to branch and weave toward higher levels of IC. However, conflict resolution strategies that do not rely on insight or self-awareness may work well for this difficult conflict partner. For example, in Chapter 1, we mentioned strategies coming out of the social approach to relationships including a practical "something for something" exchange: "You do the dishes on Sundays, and I'll wash the car." We also noted that all relationships benefit from being part of a wider social network, but that cultivating relationships to meet specific needs (for example, a friendship with a supportive person who encourages us while our loved one with a PD is unable to be encouraging) can be a good strategy for overcoming conflict in some close relationships.

Fifthly, it may be that a lifetime of giving in or compromising seems unbearable. We may need to explore in a safe context what we can bear and what we cannot. We may need to grow in self-assertiveness. Pick up the Yellow Pages. There is ample training available. We will need to learn to draw our boundaries in terms of what we will not tolerate in the relationship, and to learn how to express those new boundaries in calm and clear ways. A combination of strategies may enable us to stay in the relationship. With a bit of judicious distance, practical strategies, and more realistic expectations, relationship with a difficult person may survive and even thrive.

Sixthly, sometimes, having tried all, we reluctantly decide that living with the difficult person is not safe any longer. Our mental or physical well-being is at stake. We may need to get out. If so, we need to plan our steps wisely and confidentially. We will need a wise friend (and/or a professional) to accompany us on this journey of separation.

To separate ourselves from a difficult person does not mean that we hate them or are choosing to stew in our resentment. Forgiving the difficult person releases both parties from on-going damage. We can love them and mourn for them, but safely, protected by distance.

In sum, after trying Tit for Tat flexibly using high IC, these are the six steps to transformation through conflict with difficult people. The transformation involves a whole new way of seeing ourselves, our life, and our world, but it doesn't include our conflict partner achieving high IC.

Perhaps you are still thinking about a difficult person whom we have not yet described. They're not just different from us, they're not struggling with a PD; there's something else. Perhaps it's something to do with…

Depression and anxiety

In contrast to people with PDs, there are difficult people who know perfectly well that they are miserable. Mood disorders such as depression or anxiety are hell for the sufferer, as well as for the nearest and dearest. Depressed or anxious people are aware of their problem and are usually open to receiving help. However, their lenses on self and others are tinged with shadow and threat, making stressful events seem even more stressful. Conflict is rockier, setting off more extreme reactions of despair or fear. These people feel fragile and scared. A wise and gentle approach to conflict transformation will be needed.

Bad luck would have it that we can have a personality disorder *and* a mood disorder. We can be someone with a dependent personality *and* depression or anxiety, or all three together. Or we can have depression or anxiety on its own. Depression and anxiety are increasingly common problems;

we are ten times more likely to be depressed than our grandparents (who may have been through terrible wars, the depression of the 1930s, and the austerity years after the Second World War). It is likely that many of us will experience depression or anxiety first-hand. If not, then second-hand, through a close relationship.

In these last sections of this chapter, we focus on how people who feel depressed or anxious perceive themselves and other people. These brief sketches provide a shorthand framework that we can use to steer through conflict.

A bleak lens (depression)

Psychologist Aaron Beck[17] is famous for pinpointing the overly negative lens that people who feel depressed apply to themselves, to others, and to life in general. It's not that this bleak way of perceiving oneself and others is the cause of depression or of its accompanying paralysing sadness, lethargy, and hopelessness. But the distorted lens can reinforce the feelings of depression. It is a lens that heightens the negative:

Lens on self: I am bad, worthless, unlovable.

Lens on others: Other people are selfish, mean, angry, and don't like me.

Lens on the future: Things won't change; if they do, they will get worse.

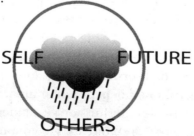

Conflict with a depressed person means "Everything looks gloomy, and this conflict is making things worse".

If we are in a conflict with a person who feels depressed, it can be hard not to catch the bleak and gloomy perspective. The conflict looks hopeless. It might be hard not to react in anger to the overly negative spin of a depressed outlook. We may feel angry that things are so tough for them and that we can't snap our fingers and make things different. Special patience may be needed to hear the depressed person's perspective. We need to practise the slow and prime steps while deploying active listening skills (see Chapter 4). Only after the depressed person knows he or she has been heard through the mirroring back of active listening can we begin to offer a different perspective that (a) accepts that this is how the depressed person is seeing things and (b) offers a more realistic picture of the situation.

Conflict transformation with a person struggling with depression may need to draw on cognitive therapy principles that are successful in treating depression. Cognitive therapy is designed to help people to examine how they are thinking about themselves, other people, and social situations. Through growing awareness of self-defeating internal scripts, people can change the scripts and start to have a more realistic lens on themselves, others, and the future. This does not seek to replace doom and gloom with rose-tinted glasses but with a healthy realism that allows for seeing both good points and bad points in themselves and others.

During conflict with a person struggling with depression, we may need to rehearse expressing our perspective in a calm way, balancing one negative statement with many positive statements. Be careful to use non-blaming, non-catastrophizing language. Avoid statements such as "This is hopeless" or "Now things will never work out" or "You're making this impossible". Try writing down in advance how to express your position and then bring that paper to the live conflict.

People struggling with depression sometimes catastrophize; a small problem feels huge and spells the end of the world. To others, it seems minor. This is a low-level IC position that can see only one perspective, and that perspective says that the whole future is bleak. If we can resist responding to their perspective in bleak terms, if we can maintain a higher-level IC position that sees both the positive and the negative, then we can help our conflict partner to come to a more realistic position regarding the issue we are arguing over. It is important that we don't overreact by denying the negative. The negatives are part of reality. So are the positives. Through the process of weaving our two conflicting viewpoints, we will come to a view that accepts that good and bad things do happen, even if we sometimes only see the bad. In this way, we will be modelling realism and hope, and these are two powerful antidotes to depression.

People struggling with depression are often helped by other forms of psychological counselling that help them to explore "why" questions. "Where did these negative views of myself and other people come from? Why can't I just shake them off? Why do some situations trigger them more than others? Why am I sometimes fine and other times unable to get out of bed?" These questions tap into the unconscious approaches to relationships mentioned in Chapter 1. Why soldier on without the help that is available? The different therapeutic approaches for depression enable a person to develop a way of perceiving themselves, others, and life itself in all their complexity of good, bad, and in-between. Counselling for people with depression aims to develop a high-level IC lens that enables them to start to enjoy the richness of life as well as accept losses and disappointments.

Some people also find a course of drug therapy for depression can be helpful in combination with counselling, especially if there are pronounced *physical* symptoms accompanying the depression (such as insomnia, lethargy, or an inability to enjoy food or sex). Research has shown that a person's brain chemistry can be altered through prolonged emotional abuse. Drugs that target certain chemicals in our brains can help to balance what the brain can no longer do for itself. There can also be genetic predispositions that are helped by drug therapies. Other people find that a course of drugs doesn't take away the symptoms but makes them manageable while they delve deeper into the "why" issues through counselling. A visit to the doctor is the first step for anyone suffering from a depression that goes on for more than a couple of weeks.

A lens attuned to danger (anxiety)
People suffering from anxiety have a lens on life that is hyper-attuned to danger. In order to survive, we all need to respond to the very real dangers of life. But the anxious person overly focuses on small threats: spiders, germs on doorknobs, enclosed spaces, social gatherings, speaking in public.[18]

It is even worse when anxiety is diffuse and generalized. It feels as if something awful is going to happen. But what? A panic attack may take hold in the supermarket. It feels as if a huge lorry is bearing down at top speed and we are going to die (fear of death may be prompting this attack). Palms sweat; heart pounds. This is the end. But we don't die. It's not a heart attack, says our doctor; it's a panic attack. So we become even more anxious that another panic attack is on its way at any moment.

This lens on life, on oneself, and on others, is a lens focused on danger. The safe aspects of life are overlooked. Conflict with an anxious person means "I am already anxious, and this conflict is making me even more afraid".

Therapy for anxiety is about enabling anxious people to face their fears while staying connected with someone who feels safe (the therapist).[19] It may take several sessions before we feel safe with a counsellor or therapist. After the relationship feels safe, gradually the counsellor or therapist will expose us to small doses of whatever is fear-producing – a rubber spider, a lift, a crowd of people. In the company of a safe and calm person, anxious people learn to connect with the safe aspects of themselves and to internalize the safety of other people. They learn to calm themselves in the face of threat. A high-level IC solution to anxiety is needed. Danger does not go away completely. Life has its dangers but there are places of safety in life.

Transforming conflict with an anxious person will require us to demonstrate that we are a safe person. Conflict is itself a threatening situation. We gently accompany the person as they face aspects of the conflict in small doses, small steps.

When alone, perhaps talking to an empty chair, we practise expressing our perspective to our anxious conflict partner in a calm, neutral way, balancing any negative statements with positive statements and using non-blaming language. Practise slow and prime with active listening skills (see Chapter 4) in order to stay calm while the anxious person is given the confidence that their perspective truly has been heard.

With an anxious person, it will be important to demonstrate that even though there is disagreement, we remain safe and faithful. Conflict does not spell the end of the relationship; we are not going to exit the relationship just because conflict has arisen. On the other side of conflict is an even more secure relationship. It's worth fighting for.

Anxious people may want an instant solution to resolve the conflict, so that they feel secure again. So, we don't rush to agreement or foreclose too early on our differences; the argument will simply erupt again. It may take time for a creative weaving of our different viewpoints to emerge. In due course, future conflicts will not be so threatening because both parties know that there is a way through. We aim to build a shared history of conflict transformation so that the relationship grows to new levels of trust and creativity.

Transformation, not magic

Whatever the distortions our lenses on ourselves and on other people, the journey toward high IC levels is in the direction of healthy psychological functioning. We start to overcome our first reaction to conflict, the blaming, shaming cry of "*You* made me do it!" As we allow our understanding to branch out, to take into consideration our own and others' perspectives, we come to understand the deep commitments that underlie our different ways of perceiving. Gradually, we find a way to weave together those different perspectives, so that something of the deep values of all parties is honoured.

IC is a necessary life skill, but it is not a magical solution. High IC is not always possible. Serious distortions of perception, feeling, and thinking (such as what can happen with the disease schizophrenia) need very different approaches (and often need medication as well as therapy).

Healthy sadness
Notice that a grieving lens is not included in a list of problematic human lenses. That is because grief is healthy. Grief is a truthful response to real loss. Grief is the necessary underbelly of love. It is so devastating and overwhelming that it can only be traversed in small steps. Hence the famous five stages of grieving: denial, anger, bargaining, depression, and, finally, acceptance.[20]

When a person is encased in grief, now is not the time to impose conflict upon them or to expect high levels of IC. They have enough to deal with. When they have navigated the process of grieving (and with enough support, however long this takes), they will have a richer, deeper, more complex experience of life that can be a resource for high-IC transformation of conflict. Those who have mourned can bring comfort to others and peace to the storm.

Questions to think about

1. How would you describe your own lens on self and other? Does either lens on self or other fit any of the sketches above? (Remember, we all have some of these

180

characteristics to some small degree.)

2. Is there a difficult person in your life?

3. Is this person simply different to you in terms of personality, in terms of how they see the world? Or is there something more going on?

4. Does this person engender conflict and difficulty with many other people or just with you?

5. How would you describe this person's lens on self and other? Does either lens on self or other fit with any of the sketches above? (Remember, we all have some of these characteristics to some small degree.)

6. How can you tailor the advice in this chapter to your difficult relationship? What seems to fit your situation? What reasonable expectations should you have regarding conflict with this person?

PART TWO

Conflict – it's between the two of you and your worlds

It's Manchester United versus Arsenal. The chanting begins. The fans in the soccer stadium split themselves down the middle. It's about loyalty to one side or the other. The tension is rising, the atmosphere is good. No goals scored yet, but game is buzzing. Suddenly – it's a goal. People stand and yell. Play goes on… No! A penalty is called – unfairly. People are booing, shouting. Someone hurls a broken bottle. A scramble begins. Your mates are at the front. This is war.

It is likely that fans on both sides are seeing the world through the low-IC eyes of threat. It is likely that brains have switched from the dominance of the neocortex's rational, higher-level thinking to the constricted, high-alert limbic processes intent on survival. The Team is at stake. Your mates are at stake. Get kicked or kick first.

This skirmish is about social identity – that is, how people answer the "Who am I?" question in terms of their group loyalties (Manchester United or Arsenal) and world views. Our self is a social self. "Don't diss my group!" That is where the threat comes in. Whatever our original baseline – high or low IC – it is the sudden plummet in IC that signals conflict. This sudden drop means "Watch out!" The situation is now one of perceived threat. What predicts violent conflict in dozens of studies is this sudden drop in IC, below the person's normal baseline.

IC, or complexity in thinking, is not the same as IQ. Winston Churchill was undoubtedly brilliant but his cognitive style was somewhat low in IC. He tended to see the world in black and white. In contrast, before the outbreak of the Second World War, British Prime Minister Neville Chamberlain demonstrated higher IC in his ability to see some of the valid political concessions that could be made to Germany in order to secure "peace in our time". But it took lower-IC Winston Churchill to perceive (rightly, in retrospect) that Hitler was a dangerous enemy who was intent on aggression, and to convince Parliament that they needed to arm, not disarm, in the face of Hitler's growing power. High IC is not always a virtue. High IC can mean there is too much information to consider or not enough clarity about where the buck stops. At times lower IC is required to respond aright to urgent threats.[1]

Like Chamberlain, some people have high IC as their general baseline, their usual way of seeing the world. To them, the world is a complex place with shades of grey and exceptions to the rule. They are hungry for more, even dissonant, information.[2] Other people, like Winston Churchill, tend to see the world more simply, more clearly, in black and white. They are settled and are not looking for new information to reshape their world view. Remember, both were prime ministers! Whatever our baseline of IC, stress, fear, and threat to important values can cause IC to plummet.

We repeat: it is not one's general baseline level of IC that spells conflict, but rather it is the *sudden drop* from the baseline that spells conflict between individuals and conflict between groups. And recall that any conflict between two individuals is also between those individuals' group world views. These world views are alive and kicking inside all our heads.

What determines the outcome is how we respond to this drop. Do we let this process run away with itself, resulting in freeze, flee, or fight? Or do we make the extra effort to raise our IC? If we make that effort, then we have the chance of regaining the full power of our social intelligence and our objective rationality. Fully equipped, we have a good chance of finding a way forward to resolve conflict in this particular situation. This has been the aim of the chapters so far.

But it is an uphill struggle. The key is, precisely, in the word "struggle". It is through the experience of struggling with conflict that we raise IC. The struggle is necessary. Research shows that struggling with a clash in opposing values provides the engine, the motivation, to see a situation afresh, to gain a new perspective that integrates even opposing viewpoints and values – in short, to raise our IC to at least level 5. This is particularly so when two values are important to us. If someone close to me has harmed me, the value of *justice* clashes with the value of *mercy*. Our value of justice cries out:

You hurt me.
This is wrong!
I've been harmed by this.
I matter.
You should be punished for this.
You should be made to suffer the way I have, so that you stop your bad behaviour.

Justice matters. But we still have a desire to see the relationship repaired. So our value of mercy also comes into play. We don't want to lose the relationship. This person matters to us. We want to find a way for the person who has hurt us to be forgiven:

Why did you do this to me? Do you know how much you hurt me?
Were you hurt in this way too, so that it seems normal to treat others like this?
What is the background to this? Are you in some problem that contributes to your bad behaviour?
How can we fix this between us?
How do you feel now that you have hurt me?
Do you feel bad? Guilty? Desperate for forgiveness?
You matter too.
Our relationship matters.
As the offended person, I am the only one who can give you the gift of forgiveness.

Mercy and compassion matter.[3]

Here is the clash. Justice demands punishment and this might destroy the relationship; mercy wants to see the relationship repaired. This is the struggle of forgiveness: the hard work of holding the perspectives of the offender and the offended in a way that meets the demands of both justice and mercy.

Sometimes forgiveness is understood as if it amounts to abandoning our own experience; as if we weren't *really* hurt, or that our perspective doesn't *really* matter. That would be too easy. Real forgiveness says clearly, "You have hurt me and that is wrong." Real forgiveness does not minimize or explain away what the offender has done. Real forgiveness does not require that we deepen our own hurt by denying what has happened to us. Sometimes the harm is permanent, and we have to face just how hurt we are. Yet, at the same time, we do not rubbish the offender as if they cannot be redeemed. We try to see beyond the label of "enemy", to perceive the real person behind the offence. We try to understand their reality, what motivated them to do what they did, and how they are feeling now. We try to see them in all their complexity. The struggle to embrace both values of justice and mercy has pressed us onwards to raise our level of IC. We struggle to grow big enough to encompass both.

Welcome to The Matrix

In Part 2, we address a further question: can anything be done to raise IC levels in society at large?

We face the profound dilemma popularized by the film *The Matrix*. How we see the world, says the film, is shaped by the fact that we, the human race, are unwittingly plugged into a vast, clandestine computer software programme that is providing all our perceptions – everything we see, hear, smell, touch. There is some truth in that wild fiction. Our minds (akin to a computer's software) are not only constructed inside our own heads; how we think is also socially constructed. We see the world through lenses that have been shaped by our cultures and world views. We see the world through the way our cultures and world views proclaim, "This is how it is."

To raise our IC, as we have seen throughout Part 1 of this book, we have to wrestle with the hard-wiring of our brains. We have to calm our primitive limbic system in order to get beyond the binary world of freeze, flee, or fight. There is also a social aspect to low IC, as described in Chapter 3 (My group made me do it). Now, in Part 2, we expand on that social aspect. Our task is not only to struggle with our brain's hard-wiring. We also have to struggle with the socially shared thinking systems (cultures and world views), which, like a computer's software, shape how we think.

Isn't a person's general cognitive style, low or high in complexity, fixed in stone? What good will it do to struggle with the software of our world views? The answer to this broader question is answered by recent research. There is, for all people, a natural developmental pathway from simplicity to complexity. It is natural for human beings to progress from thinking in simple ways toward thinking in more complex ways. There may be a slightly different upper limit on this for each individual. However, we rarely attain all our capacity, either individually or socially. We can *always* push our IC levels higher.

Human beings are natural scientists, natural meaning-makers. We all want to understand what is going on in the world, what our life is about. Yet this pathway toward complexity can be stunted by experiences that traumatize us, or by social conditions that oppress us. Our baseline IC levels can be stunted by social world views that don't allow us to grow.

Just how deep does the rabbit hole go?

Large institutions, organizations, and ideologies often operate through efficient, low-IC ways. When people sign up to their organization's particular world view, those who are low-IC, fit in well. They have joined the in-group. They know who is in and who is out, and how to enforce the rules that govern that division. People whose world is in black and white are fairly predictable. Organizations know what will make them react, what will make them angry, what will make them pleased. Similarly, advertisers know (to some extent) what will make them buy which product.

In contrast, people who are high-IC have more options in how they see the world, and this gives them more choices and greater internal freedom. They can be harder to predict, harder to control. Thus, they are not always the most popular kid on the street. For some large institutions and ideologies, there is something subversive about high-IC thinking. Many times in human history, high-IC thinking has been actively suppressed. Humanity inevitably started out thinking in simple terms and then grew from there. Yet sometimes we are pressured to return to those earlier states. Sometimes that pressure is social.

Starting out very simple

The sociologist Emile Durkheim[4] noted that primitive tribes require "sameness" at each level of the tribe's segments. In order for the tribe to function, each group in society has to hold similar beliefs and attitudes. Whether a person is a fisherman, hunter, or clay pot maker, everyone needs to see reality in the same way. In a tribe headed by a chief carrying sacred status, only one point of view is allowed, only one single reality can be upheld: the chief's. Under primitive conditions, a tribe would cease to function if people started to do their own thing. Everyone's world view had to be glued (fused) to the world view of the all-powerful chief. So, maintaining the beliefs and world view of the chief was paramount, as seen in a researcher's account of an isolated tribe. A young man, a tribal member, accidently farted in the chief's sacred presence. The sacred order had been defiled. The young man immediately left the chief's hut, climbed up a tall tree, and threw himself on to the sharpened stakes below.

From fused oneness to the opposed two
The long and winding road of civilization has led us beyond fused, tribal world views toward greater complexity. We advanced from a fused world ruled by god-kings and tyrants to the modern world. But before 1989 this was a world split between two nuclear superpowers. The superpowers eyeballed each other with intense suspicion. Each superpower, Western or Communist, believed the other was out to destroy. Both were committed to protecting themselves through nuclear deterrence: arsenals of such overkill that no one in their right mind would start a nuclear war. It was MAD – Mutually Assured Destruction. Somehow we survived more than sixty years as a world riven by a two-fold split. Although this binary, two-fold world was still relatively low-IC (us versus them), it was an advance beyond the primitive state of fused world views.

In a world made up of two giant superpowers, it made sense to think at relatively low levels of IC, reflecting the feeling of the world being split between two camps. Each superpower (with their contrasting forms of government) had its own top dogs and lower echelons. Each formed its own pyramid of power. Each side said to the other, "We are right; you are wrong. We are the good guys; you are the bad guys. We are only trying to defend our way of life; you are out to attack us." The Cold War dragged on thus until one of the players collapsed from exhaustion.

From the opposed two to a complex interrelated plurality
Then the Berlin Wall came down. Post-1989, the pyramid-shaped, two-fold world began to melt into spread-out horizontal networks as nations crumbled, rearranged themselves, and formed new alliances that cut across the old

binaries. Trade boomed. Democracy spread. The internet exploded the rate and quantity of transfer of goods and information. "Tiger economies" zoomed into prosperity. The free-trade recipe for prosperity was adopted, and modified, into cultures of the Far East.

As the world has morphed into a networked, fluid, IT, "virtual" shape, so too has the number of threats: climate change, terrorism from a wide array of extremisms, failed states, mass migrations, financial crises. We now live in an increasingly complex social world. Different cultures and religions are rubbing shoulders in new ways. But has our cognitive and moral development, our ability to think about the world in which we live, kept pace? Or are our world views still, socially, low-IC?

As always, we internalize the contours of the social world we live in. It takes some time for our internal, subjective world views to change. Christian dissident Richard Wurmbrandt gave voice to this, saying that he had been in communist prisons for fifteen years, but it took another fifteen years for communist prisons to come out of him.[5] It takes even longer for socially shared world views to change: more people have to get on board the train for change.

We are in a new situation, but very often old binary ways of thinking carry on, even though they no longer serve us as well. Our current socially shared world view is still constructed on various binary splits. Raising our IC levels has become more necessary than ever if humanity is to solve the complex problems of our globalized condition. Given that raising our IC levels is always hard work, what cultural support will give humanity's IC levels the best chance to rise on a widespread scale? How can we raise the IC of the world views we inhabit, especially if they are enticing us to continue in low-IC ways?

Our desire to raise our own IC levels may be motivated simply by our personal relationship disasters and conflicts. We want happy relationships. End of story. Yet, whether we like it or not, we are like Neo in *The Matrix*. Our own IC levels are connected to a larger thinking system. If we change ourselves, we begin to change something bigger. We start to rattle the bigger cage. (Yes, it will resist this.) If we don't challenge the outdated binaries, the larger world-view system will entice us back to low IC.

In the next chapters, ways of raising our own IC in concert with the IC of our wider culture and world view are presented. How we parent, teach, organize our work lives, and how we think about politics, science, and religious faith are among the most powerful shapers of human consciousness. These great socializing forces have shaped us and our IC levels. In these final chapters we focus on the impact these forces have had upon us personally (Chapter 6). Now we turn the tables, and we start to shape them, even where it seems impossible (Chapter 7). The core life skill of IC (summarized in Chapter 8) can help us to recapture our natural impetus toward complexity in order to meet the startlingly new challenges to our survival and flourishing.

CHAPTER 6

My parents made me do it

Don't tell me what to do. Please could you do this homework for me? Hey, Dad, look at me! Keep out – it's my room. I can't find my shoes. *Love me, help me, and leave me alone.*

Parents have the complex task of responding to the push and pull of their children's infinite needs. Parents are our first experience of "how to do relationships". Through what our parents model, parents resource us – or under-resource us – to engage with other people in all their complexity.

Yet parents' first task is to ensure the survival and safety of their child. It's an emergency! When survival is at stake, parents may have to sacrifice complex thinking for emergency thinking. If this happens over the long haul, parents inevitably will be modelling lower levels of IC for their children. If, however, conditions allow for flourishing, parents then have more flexibility in how they raise their children. And how they do this has profound implications for how well children adapt to the complex society we now live in.

Thousands of studies have been carried out in the last twenty years on the effects of different parenting styles. A growth industry in the West, the evidence is overwhelming. In advanced consumerist, Western-influenced societies, *give and take* parenting, which balances supportive, involved caring with firm boundaries and expectations, has the most positive outcomes for the child. From these studies we can identify four main parenting styles: *give and take, boss, whatever you want*, and *I don't care*.

Reflecting on what we experienced in our own upbringing will shed light on how we personally handle relationship conflict and what our own strengths and weaknesses are. How we parent our own children and teach or mentor younger people will equip, or not, the next generation to deal with the complexities of life. Armed with the bigger picture, we can make informed choices about how we aim to influence the next generation. We can shape the shapers that will form the next generation. In Chapter 4, we offered reflective questions that focused on familiar experiences of conflict. With the following snapshots of parenting styles, we continue that process of self-discovery. Read through the following descriptions while thinking about (a) what you experienced while growing up, and (b) how you interact with your children, children in your care, or young people in your life.

1. "Give and take" parenting
(called *authoritative parenting* in the parenting literature[1])

Mother: Have you done your homework?

Child: No, I'll do it later. I want to play at Heidi's.

Mother: And when might later be?

Child: Later. I want to go play at Heidi's. Pleeeeeeze. I want to...

Mother: OK, I can see you really want to – so you can go and play at Heidi's for a while, but you have to come back by four o'clock.

Child: Why? I don't want to.

Mother: You have to be back by four o'clock so that you do your homework before dinner. I will collect you at four. But for now, go and have fun with Heidi.

In the above snippet of *give and take* parenting, the parent is warm and able to take the child's perspective: the child really wants to play at Heidi's. In addition, the parent has clear standards and places firm boundaries. The parent is both supportive and demanding. The child's homework must be done.

Give and take parenting retains the responsible adult perspective at all times, yet without crushing the child's feelings, thoughts, and desires. In this way, *give and take* parenting shows relatively high IC. It's about taking both the adult perspective and the child's perspective, and integrating these, moment by moment. This takes a lot of work. Integration means that the child's own thoughts, feelings, and wishes are engaged with, while the parents continue to act in the child's best interests. In this snippet, a *give and take* compromise solution is found: the child can have some time playing and an adequate amount of time for homework.

In *give and take* parenting, the parent shows that both the parent and the child have the right to be listened to; both have the right to be treated with respect. It's a two-way street. The adult retains full responsibility at all times, yet does not act as a "brick wall". In this way, children grow up with a sense of their own personhood and their own perspective, while knowing that they can't expect always to have their own way. Parents and teachers often have the final say. The child has early experience that life entails different perspectives: their own and others'.

In the West (and Western-influenced countries), *give and take* parenting results in children who do well in school and have fewer problems such as truancy or vandalism. Young people raised in this way tend to get good jobs and are generally able to face and solve problems. They do well in life. Children raised with this kind of parenting have a sense of self. They know who they are. They know they have a valid perspective. These children have been gifted with a foundation for high IC levels and conflict resolution. They own their own perspective as valid. They also know that others have different perspectives, that these too are valid and worth listening to.

This parenting style provides a good match with what is now required for success within our fluid, consumer society. No more does the obeisance of the assembly line lackey – who doffs his cap when the boss walks by – spell success. Contemporary culture calls for independent, creative, flexible, problem-solving, conflict-resolving young people to work collaboratively in IT, science, medicine, communication, the arts. And the research shows that *give and take* parenting now best serves this end. Indeed, the *give and take*, authoritative parenting style is considered the norm in the West; it is spoken of as "positive parenting" (meaning everything else is "negative"). Glance at the shelves of parenting magazines for sale and you will see this model in operation. But we should be clear that it is positive because it works well in our current globalized, fluid context.

*Conflict with the child of **give and take** parents*

Ben learned early on that his parents would negotiate with him whenever he had fights with them. Sometimes Ben would rebel just to see how much he could get away with. But his parents would hold firm and would carry on with long explanations until Ben came around.

Sometimes his parents would say, "Just go to your room and think about it for while." While in his own room, Ben would have the space to think up ways to try to get his own way. In the quiet, he came to know his own thoughts and what was really important to him. He tried to imagine what his parents would say in response. He began to be able to guess what position they would take and how to counter this. In his family, arguments could be talked about for a very long time until everyone came around. Usually there would be some creative solution that made sense even to Ben.

Ben got along with his family on the whole, but he did have some fights at school. Ben's dad was helping him learn how to stand his own ground with the school bully. Apart from the bully, school was OK. Ben knew that he needed to try his hardest to get good grades; otherwise his parents would have more long talks with him. His favourite times were in track and field; Ben could really run. He could beat everyone in the races. But it was different with his best friend, James. James had diabetes and had to have injections every day. Sometimes James was sick and couldn't do much in sports. Ben never bragged in front of him or egged him on to race him. They just got on and did other things that were fun.

In this cameo, it looks as if Ben will emerge into adulthood with the idea that the world around him will adapt to him to some degree; he will have the confidence to make his mark. He will be able to stand his own ground. Ben has been helped by his parents to face up to powerful people who disagree with him (or attack him, like the school bully). Having this ability to see others as separate, real people with their own separate views, Ben also feels compassion for people who suffer, such as his best friend, James. Ben is able to be sensitive to others' feelings. He knows when to brag, when to be quiet, when to compete, and when not to. Because Ben has had experience of *give and take*, firm boundaries, and that win–win solutions to conflicts are possible, he can enter into conflict with an ability to hang on to his own perspective. He is able to be interested in the perspectives of others; sometimes others have greater wisdom. It will be relatively smooth sailing for Ben to discover different conflict styles (direct, avoid, compromise, accommodate, collaborate) and different ways of integrating opposing perspectives. Conflict means "This is a challenge, not a disaster".[2]

If this describes our own upbringing, we can thank our parents for the serendipity of an upbringing that happened to connect with the fast-paced changes of Western culture. If this describes how we are interacting with those in our care, we're doing fine. To this style, we can also add, in judicious amounts, other parenting styles (described in the next sections), depending upon the context, for a truly high-IC approach.

2. *"Here comes the **boss**" parenting*
(Called *authoritarian* in the literature[3])
Here, the parent is the *boss*. *Boss* parenting is common in traditional, communal, tightly knit, hierarchical societies around the world. This parenting style is still somewhat

common in many Western and Western-influenced societies. Certainly, before the social revolution of the 1960s, authoritarian *boss* parenting was the dominant mode of child-rearing in most cultures.

Boss parents care intensely about their children and want the best for their children. The parent simply has the final word. So, there is little give and take in communication between parent and child here. *Boss* parents are often generous to the point of sacrifice. But *boss* parents tell their children what to do. Communication is one-way.

Mother: Have you done your homework?

Child: I'll do it later. I want to go to Heidi's.

M: No, you have to do your homework.

Child: But I really want to...

M: I told you to do your homework; you need to improve your spelling...

Child: But I can do it later...

M: Now, I said. Do your homework now.

You are unlikely to hear an authoritarian *boss* parent asking for the child's perspective or entering into the reasons why a dress of a certain length may or may not be worn. The answer is "Because I say so". This is how conflict is resolved. Even so, the impact on offspring is not necessarily bad news. It can work well, producing disciplined, dutiful, and often affectionate children.

When *boss* parents are warm, this helps the child to be able to "read" the parents' basic motives. Still, the child knows not to argue back. It can be difficult for children when even well-meaning *boss* parents are cool and reserved. They are thus harder to read. Either way, whether warm or cool in the expression of affection, *boss* parents are more absolute in their discipline: "Do as I say!" The parent is always right. They will punish the child without question when the rules are broken. They demand, and usually get, respect.

This style of parenting can result in young people who are not accustomed to owning their own perspective. They may be less aware of their own thoughts and feelings because what counts are the thoughts and feelings of the parents or other powerful people. These young people will have less experience in integrating their own perspective with the perspectives of others. Those in authority are always right. The child may remain glued to the parent's perspective as they grow up, or they may rebel when they enter the terrible teens. They may then become demanding, authoritarian adults, following in their parents' footsteps. Whether they acquiesce or demand their own way, it will require new socializing input to enable young people raised in this way to integrate their own perspectives with those of others. They will be less well prepared for the give and take of the new multicultural, networked, fluid, make-it-up-as-you-go-along society.

Conflict with the child of **boss** parents

Sharon was raised by strict parents who wanted her to do well. Her parents took her everywhere, to school, church, shopping, relatives' homes. Her parents were always there, the bedrock of life, keeping the standards, making sure all was well. Being polite really mattered. Sharon wasn't allowed to raise her voice or talk back. Not that there were any big fights; Sharon knew what the rules were and that these had to be obeyed. Home life was quiet and well ordered. Sharon had to get good grades, do her chores. She would be rewarded with lovely clothes. To get around the rules meant that Sharon had to do this without being noticed. Sharon gradually became reserved at home and spent most of her time in her room listening to music.

When she was out with her friends, Sharon was a different girl: funny, wild, daring. She would change her hair and dress style from one week to the next. It was as if she was experimenting with her own image of herself, trying to discover her own personality. Her political views changed every week too. There was always a new cause for Sharon to defend. This week it was "Save the bees". At home, she buried all this fight and clamour; there just wasn't space for it.

Sharon was popular at school, but her friends learned not to fight with her. Arguments ended in breakups. Anyone who tried to beat Sharon in an argument found that she would ignore them from that point on. She wasn't good at listening to the other side because it felt overwhelming to her. Conflict for Sharon means "Don't threaten me. I have to defend my corner in order to survive".

It may seem that Sharon's parents "made her do it". Yes, they are part of a cocktail of influences. But if Sharon's experience of *boss* parenting had been close and intimate, if Sharon had a temperament more suited to closeness, perhaps she would have emerged into young adulthood with a more accommodating approach to conflict: "Let's do it your way." Both responses have strengths and weaknesses. The reality is that no parenting style utterly determines what happens in a person's life. Human life is a soup with many ingredients. Each individual brings their own temperament, personality, and gifts, along with a host of other influences from school, friends, wider culture. There are a number of ways for a person with Sharon's upbringing to go in response to conflict: avoid, direct, accommodate, compromise, and even collaborate.

Nevertheless, it seems likely that children of *boss* parents will have less experience in voicing their own perspective at home and thus may be less good at doing this with other people. They may be less good at listening to others' perspectives without feeling overwhelmed or needing to rebel. None of this is fixed in stone. Under the right conditions, the skills of integrating one's own and others' perspectives can be learned, though this is never easy.

If this sounds like our own experience of being parented, or of how we parent or mentor children and young people, there are positives as well as some negatives. Despite the relative drawbacks of *boss* parenting for preparing children to enter the fluid nature of society today, authoritarian parenting does help to build the self-discipline needed to learn IC in later life, if they are motivated to do so.

*3. "**Whatever you want**, darling" parenting*
(called *permissive* parenting[4])
Whatever you want, indulgent parents take great care over their children. Like *give and take* or *boss* parents, they too care intensely for their children. Here, however, the parents require little in return. The child's perspective is all-important. Parents do not impose rules and boundaries.

Mother: Have you done your homework?

Child: I'll do it later. I want to play at Heidi's.

Mother: Oh that's nice – you can go and play at Heidi's, but you will have to decide whether you are going to do your homework today.

Child: I'll do it later. Don't nag me.

Mother: I'm not nagging you! You can go and play.

It was hoped that children reared with the new permissive parenting experiment would grow up into confident and creative young people. Sadly, the permissive parenting experiment that began in the 1960s – "Whatever you want, darling, you must decide for yourself" – has not had positive outcomes. Children's grades suffer, their lives as adults suffer. Although *whatever you want* parents are very concerned with their child's feelings and thoughts, they do not integrate these with a responsible adult perspective. In this way, we could say that permissive, *whatever you want* parenting models a lower level of IC than *give and take* parenting.

Conflict with the child of **whatever you want** parents

Tammy took centre stage in the life of her parents. Whatever it was that Tammy wanted, Tammy got: tap-dancing lessons, roller blades, sparkly pink nail polish, sleepovers with friends, extra tuition when she struggled in school. She wasn't made to do things she didn't want to do. She was told she needed to make her own mind up about religion, about politics. When she didn't want to eat the dinner placed before her, her mother made some other food. Apart from her tantrums, Tammy remembers her childhood as a happy time. Her childhood memories are mainly populated with herself and the things she wanted to do. It was great fun.

But now that Tammy is at university, her parents are no longer around to meet her every need. It seems an unfair blow to Tammy to find that other people are quite unsympathetic to her. Other people seem unkind, demanding, and unhelpful. Tammy finds that she rubs other people up the wrong way. She is told that she always whines and always wants things her own way. To Tammy, other people's demands on her seem unreasonable. If Tammy feels she can win, conflict means "My way!"; otherwise, Tammy will avoid, and do things on her own.

Children raised by permissive, *whatever you want* parents get a real shock when they enter adult life. They may expect to have things their own way – it was ever thus. As children, they simply did not have the experience of negotiating with other people's perspectives. Other children of permissive parents might be *unable* to stand up for their rights; their parents did that for them. The school of hard knocks feels overwhelming and cruel. They need a protector. Conflict can also mean "I'll tell my daddy on you!"

This may describe some of us. And this may make sense of some of the recurring patterns in our own relationship conflicts. Our parents meant well. They dutifully read the latest books on parenting (misguided as these turned out to be). Whatever parenting styles we have experienced, most of us find ourselves in the place of being a hinge generation: "This is what I experienced; I am going to do it differently." The key to being different is to be consciously aware of both the positives and negatives of our own experience. It is reactive simply to do the opposite of our own parents' style.

A high-IC approach picks and chooses the best from a wider range of parenting styles.

4. *"I don't care" parenting*
(called *neglectful* parenting[5])

I don't care, neglectful parents take very little active participation in the child's life. Neither the child's perspective nor the responsible adult perspective really matters. Parents give their children freedom without rules to contain them. Parents are unresponsive to their children's wishes and needs, and they have few expectations of them in return. The outcome for children's flourishing is bleak. They may grow up lacking self-discipline and a sense of who they are. They may not even get their basic needs met (such as enough food, clothing, hygiene, or shelter).

> John comes home from school. His mother is watching television.
>
> He throws his school books down and shouts, "I hate all this homework!"
>
> His mother turns up the television volume.

In this snippet, it doesn't matter what John does. His homework and his feelings don't really matter. His mother avoids the adult perspective she should be taking. No doubt there will be a sad story behind her lack of parenting skills. Her lack of effort to integrate her child's perspective with her own responsible adult perspective means that John has no safe container: no one to belong to, no one to shape him. This parenting style is an even lower IC level than *boss* or *whatever you want* parenting. Neither perspectives of child or parent are taken into account. Low IC is modelled to the developing child who soaks up their environment like a sponge. The child is underprepared for life and work in a world requiring creativity and discipline, a world in which many perspectives need to be negotiated.

*Conflict with children of **I don't care** parents*

> John's life is without rules. At times it is chaotic. He's lived with his grandmother, and then back again with his mother. He's never been able to settle into a school for long. He gets kicked out and then goes back in, but he has never been able to master his reading. Not that anyone has noticed. So he keeps himself entertained by being the leader of his own gang. Sometimes he gets caught and is called a bully. What does it matter? Actions and consequences didn't really line up in childhood, so who knows what to expect? Conflict means "Whatever. Who cares?"; fight, give up, or avoid.

Statistics concerning his future are not on John's side. Yet there is something remarkable about human potential. The serious disadvantage of neglect can be overcome, at least by some people. Inner resilience combined with a degree of support from others (however peripheral – a caring grandparent, an inspiring teacher, a helpful counsellor) can overturn all gloomy predictions. In fact, an important early marker of potential leadership is parental loss, particularly the loss of a father in early childhood. According to one British study,[6] over 60 per cent of major British political leaders lost a parent in childhood, more often the father. The annals of *Who's Who* are overpopulated with orphans. It may be that children living with one or both parents are content to take their social cues from their mother or father, whereas those who have lost one or both parents are forced to design their own goals and values. Without parents, these children have to become their own model. Unable to depend on others, they have learned to depend on themselves. But this happens in conjunction with the explicit encouragement, investment of time, and love from an adult, *somehow*. Children without any adult care grow up very disturbed.

If this feels a familiar story to some of us, we have done very well indeed to be where we now are. It will not have been easy. We will not wish to inflict this kind of neglect on anyone.

These four different styles of parenting (*boss, give and take, whatever you want,* and *I don't care*) can be mapped in a similar way to leadership styles and conflict styles described in Chapter 4.

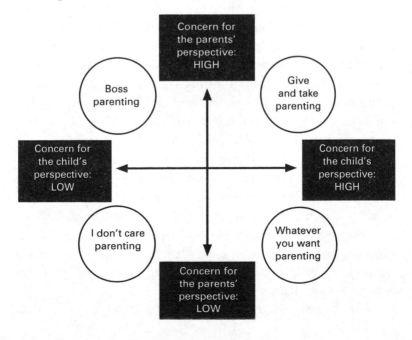

Parents model how to do it (not "make" you do it)

The evidence is overwhelming that *give and take* parenting usually shows the best outcomes in Western-influenced cultures. Yet there may be times when a truly flexible parent takes a different approach now and then. To do this, we offer a two-step guide.

First, we need to be able to rise to high IC, being concerned for both our adult/parental *and* child's perspectives. Second, we need to develop the capacity to assess which parenting style to use at this particular moment, in this context, with these relationships. A medical emergency may not be a good moment in which to canvas our child's opinion. We simply act, authoritatively, in their best interests. In other contexts, we may decide to give in, permissively, to our child. Perhaps the child's fear of incessant bullying at school is so intense that we realize that, for now, they need home schooling, despite the disruption it will cause to our schedule. Even the much-praised *give and take*, "positive parenting" style needs to show some flexibility, at least some of the time. We might say that at times a parent can discern a long-term perspective beneath their own or the child's short-term preferences and act for the long-term good, even if it disrupts short-term life.

A degree of flexibility and sensitivity toward the child that takes into consideration the context enables megahigh-IC parents to adapt their parenting style to nurture the child in the midst of ever-changing needs and challenges. This approach to parenting models a wide range of skills to the children. Children are good at picking up underlying, unwritten rules. This is how they learn language. They do it easily. They internalize these unwritten rules, and the rules become second nature to them.

For the parents, this hardly adds up to an easy life. This

megahigh-IC parenting is a very high-level skill, requiring that ability to stand back and observe self and others in the dynamic interplay. And parents will make mistakes all the time. That's OK. Being high-level IC enables them to acknowledge their mistakes so that parent and child can learn together.

Let's connect our approach to conflict with parenting. Each conflict style represents an integration of our concern for relationships and our concern for the task at hand. The various ways we can integrate these concerns leads to identifiably different conflict styles. For example, a directing style is concerned for the relationship (even though this is not so obviously the director's first priority) as the relationship can contribute to accomplishing the task at hand (the priority). Here, a parent is concerned that their relationship with their child helps the child get a good education (high concern for the task). In contrast, an accommodating conflict style is concerned also for the task as it can contribute to maintaining the relationship (the priority for accommodators). Here, a parent is concerned that the child washes the dinner dishes and puts them away as a way of contributing to family life. A compromising style is somewhat concerned for both the task and relationship as it facilitates fair play amongst all parties to the conflict. A parent teaches siblings to negotiate who chooses the DVD on a Friday night so that each child learns about fair play. A collaborating style is highly concerned for both the task and relationship as it facilitates maximum creativity and exploration of innovative options. A parent sets up an art table challenging each child to create a spaceship from the materials available in thirty minutes, rewarding the most creative design with half an hour playing their favourite computer game. And an avoiding style is initially concerned with getting enough time and space to reflect on the task and relationship. A parent ignores a child's grumbling while walking from the museum to the car; upon reflection the parent recognizes that the child is tired and hungry, thus grumpy. An avoider might then move into another conflict style, possibly a directing style (to get food). Yet, also concerned that the relationship supports the task at hand, a parent might firmly and lovingly direct the child toward a hot meal, bath, and bed, despite cries of protest, knowing the child will awaken in a better mood.

The ideal parenting goal is to be able to assess a conflict in order to adapt the conflict style most appropriate to that situation, rather than to react from our default conflict style. By assessing the context, the task or issue, and the adults and children involved, we make a measured judgment about which conflict style to use. We may need to be a Winston Churchill now and then, and face aggressors head on (directing style): "Punching your sister is not allowed – that's final!" Sometimes we avoid, giving everyone some time and space. We overhear siblings squabble and decide to let them sort it out rather than intervene. Sometimes we compromise, aiming for fair play: "No, you promised your brother a turn, so it's his turn now." Sometimes we collaborate, reaching for creativity and innovation: "Let's see, how can you both enjoy this one toy at the same time? Any ideas?" Sometimes you accommodate, affirming the relationship before moving into problem-solving. "Jimmy, you know I love you very much. You want to play your computer games and I know you need to do your homework. So how can we sort this out together?" Integrating the various approaches to conflict is very high IC, a learned capacity to move around all the conflict styles as required by the context.

Parents are not all-powerful, and, as already suggested,

every parenting style will interact with the child's own temperament. A very strong-willed child will learn from *give and take* parenting, just like any child, but they may need some extra insight into their own and others' perspectives. With a toddler throwing a tantrum, a very effective response involves holding the child in our arms in a loving but very firm embrace while they flay about. Eventually we will feel their little bodies go limp. A tantrum may be an expression of an inner panic at feeling alone or not feeling "contained" in a safe environment. This does not mean that we are not parenting well. The triggers can be hidden and ultimately undetermined. Consistent and immediate physical holding, an expression of loving containment and presence, eventually penetrates the toddler's panic. They internalize a feeling of safety: they are not alone in their terror. As they grow older, consistent, loving boundaries will provide the safe environment for a strong-willed child to assert themselves without walking over everyone else. Careful explanations of family rules and consequences for breaking the rules, open to questioning, discussion, and perhaps some negotiation will create a safe environment for the child to continue to express their will while learning to consider other perspectives.

If a parent mainly views their child as an extension of themselves, this can lead to the use of force or control with their children. This is can be hard to avoid completely, especially if the parent and child share very evident physical and personality similarities: "Oh no, my child is me!" The parents see their own self-worth as dependent upon their children's performance. They want their children to take advantage of opportunities they never had. Their child must hold up the family honour. If high-IC parenting is a goal, then it becomes much harder to achieve this if the parent is not a connected *and* separate person. To enable our children to become adept at perceiving their own perspectives and those of others, we have to make a similar journey for ourselves. This journey will enable us to respect the child's perspective, even when we disagree with it.

From the flow of our argument, it becomes clear that force and control can become abusive. The long-term destructive outcomes of all forms of child abuse (verbal, emotional, physical, and sexual) has been well researched.[7] It is often in the news. A parent completely absorbed by their own needs will lash out at a child who is bounding around with noisy exuberance or making a ruckus in order to draw some attention and adult interaction. Rather than understanding the child's needs, the parent inflicts abuse to force the child to be what the parent wants in that moment: silent, invisible, unmoving, undemanding. With repetition, the child's perspective narrows down to mere survival. Both parent and child are hurting, but the child cannot protect themselves. The person who is supposed to care for them is hurting them. This can be called *I will hurt you* parenting. The level of IC for this parenting style is in the red (negative). In abusive parenting, the parent trashes both the child and their own parental responsibility. Sadly, the child blames themselves, feels ashamed, and internalizes a level of self-hatred. Gentle play therapy can help them to express their pent-up terror and rage. No longer blaming themselves, they can start to see their own and others' perspectives outside the lenses of abuse.

By recognizing the influences in our own lives that may have enabled us to see the world through high-IC eyes (respecting our own and others' points of view, and even integrating several viewpoints), we begin to see how we can empower the next generation. Perhaps we feel that our upbringing has more disabled than enabled high IC levels. We can grieve this, but it is never too late to learn how to raise our own IC. When we exercise high IC with our children or those we mentor, we gain back something of what we lost out on. Wherever we find ourselves just now, our shared task as adults is to be, as described earlier, a hinge generation; people who enable the next generation to learn from our experiences. It seems very likely that young people today will face conflicts even more complex than we have faced in the past decades. Preparing them for the future will be as easy and as hard as doing unto others what you would have them do unto you.

Questions to think about

1. Which parenting style(s) best describe your parents or carers?
2. Did both parents/carers use the same parenting style? Was one parent, for example, authoritarian ("Here comes the boss"), and the other parent indulgent ("Whatever you want, darling")? Were you aware of this as a child, or are you seeing this now for the first time?
3. What is/are your usual conflict style(s)? (See Chapter 4,conflict styles self-discovery quiz.)
4. Are there any links between the kind of parenting you experienced and how you approach conflict?
5. If you are a parent, in a parenting role, or work with young people, are you following the parenting style

of your parents/carers, or are you reworking what was modelled to you into a different style?

In what cultural context is your child, young person in your care, or the young people you work with growing up? What will they need to succeed? How can you enable and empower them to have the personal resources for the future they will face?

School

The next big shaper in our lives, after our parents, is school. Educators used to be mysterious, all-knowing beings who filled up, from on high, empty containers (pupils) with knowledge. Communication was one-way, similar to *boss* parenting. This approach is now considered poor teaching practice, and modern teaching is much more sensitive to the child's level of readiness for new knowledge as well as their learning style. Modern teaching practice is interactive. Integrating the child's natural interests with their learning style and the skills and information needed for successful living, it seeks to draw out understanding from pupils, beginning at the child's level and then supporting them to reach a little higher.[8] At its best, it is high IC.

Only since the 1960s have schools, colleges and universities in the West begun to require students to write and argue from multiple perspectives on assigned topics and to weave together opposing perspectives. Thus, even in the West, encouraging young people to aim for high IC is a relatively new thing, both in parenting and in school.

If our teachers taught us from on high, with little interest in our perspective, asking us only to parrot the right answer, it is unlikely that we, as students, were able to develop much voice to interact with theirs. High IC was not modelled. We simply had to get through and get out. Only if we were lucky did we get an education that prepared us to deal with opposing perspectives and to live in a multicultural world with its fast-changing world of work. If we are teaching today, we will be working at empowering young people to achieve high IC for themselves. This is something to hang on to when the context of our teaching becomes stressful or demoralizing. We are at the cutting edge, shaping the next shapers.

Did your teachers encourage you to give the "right" answers or to see different perspectives? How was disagreement handled? Did you see one conflict style at work or several? How has your school experience shaped your ability to see other points of view and your conflict style(s)?

Work

Similarly, until very recently, many employers or managers had a *boss* leadership style. At the end of the day, it was the profit margin that provided the bottom line, and that was non-negotiable. Bosses and managers needed to be good at the task; good social skills in handling people were not required. Over time, research started to suggest that it was helpful for leaders (in the military, in business, in professions) also to be good with people.[9] People needed to be treated as human beings in order for them to do a good job. The best leaders, said the new management science, should integrate their concern for the job at hand with their concern for people in a way that empowers the people and gets the job done. High IC. *Boss*-led organizations began moving toward integrating perspectives of management and labour (such as cooperatives). Some of these flatter, more egalitarian organizations – such as Infosys Technologies, ICICI Bank, OneWorld Health, and Four Seasons Hotels[10] – encourage worker creativity with enormous success. Everyone, from "empowering" bosses (who mentor employees to fully develop their abilities) through to the tea boy, needs the ability to deal with conflicting perspectives at work.

Using high IC at work today means many layers of integration: the perspective of the work that needs to be done with the perspectives of those doing the work; the perspective of the internal organizational context with the perspective of the external organizational context, its competitors and particular field of enterprise; the perspectives of the larger economic and financial contexts with those of the political and social contexts; and all of these with each other into an overarching "meta" perspective. High IC at work sometimes means affirming the people more than the task, as in a recession when business can be slow and time can be used to retrain and develop employee skills for the emerging economy. Being a high-IC manager means we take multiple perspectives in conflict and empower others to advance in their own careers. When we go up the ladder ourselves, we seek to take others with us. Whatever our role in the organization, when we are in conflict with colleagues or our managers at work, we need to bring all these perspectives into our efforts at conflict transformation. Whoever said work was easy?

Do your work supervisors, committee chairs, volunteer or team leaders (these might be you!) insist on one viewpoint, or are different perspectives allowed and even incorporated into short-, medium- and long-term plans for the way forward? How is disagreement handled? Do you see one conflict style or several at work? How is your work (paid or unpaid) experience shaping your ability to see other perspectives and your conflict style(s)?

The shape of things to come

Some extremely fortunate people have experienced high-IC *give and take* parenting, some high-IC interactive teaching, and some high-IC empowering leadership in their (paid or unpaid) work experience. If this describes us, then situations involving conflict with authority or opposing perspectives may be stressful but not terminal. We have the personal resources (along with the tools and skills in this book) to work through, even transform conflict. We find we do not lose a sense of ourselves as a person, collapsing into a fearful, gibbering wreck, nor do we have to fight so hard to get some power for ourselves that we become ruthless and manipulative. People who can face conflicts at work in this way are considered to be naturally self-assertive. Nature may have gifted them with strong temperaments and sensitivity to other people, but so too have parents, teachers, and employers.

Generation Y – young people born between the 1980s and 2000 – are the children of parents who went through the social changes of the 1960s. These young people take for granted that their own perspective counts. No good expecting

Generation Y to put up and shut up. Young people know their rights. They can always have their say on Facebook, YouTube, Twitter. They can text friends, join a chat room, send photos or film clips. Young people are multimedia communicators. Even political power has become more immediate, more permeable to the person on the street. A young person, capturing a video on their mobile phone, which, for example, implicates a policeman in using excessive force, can upload that footage on to the internet in seconds. Popular uprisings against dictators can no longer be denied as if they never happened – the footage is on YouTube.

This is the shape of things to come. The pyramid-shaped world is melting into a flatter network as globalization proceeds. The democratic way, which gives all people a voice, is pervading every aspect of human relationships. We help it along by wielding high IC in our own small corner. We are like Neo, taking down the Matrix, bit by bit.

This leads us to our last frontier – the shaper of shapers – religion.

CHAPTER 7

My religion made me do it

Defend your kingdom, O God. Give me the strength of purpose to fight against those who oppose you, those who ignore the exhortations of your chosen vessel. Give me the strength to proclaim truth to those who will listen – to those who are among the community of the saved.

We get hot under the collar when we hear religious language like this. Many of us are eager to rush to low IC where religion is concerned. Historian Samuel Huntingdon struck a chord with some (and enfuriated others) when he proclaimed that the new binary split marking the twenty-first century takes the form of a "clash of civilizations".[1] A key feature of this clash, he argues, is religious.

Whatever our view of religion, we're living through this clash and it affects how we experience conflict in our relationships at home, work, in our community and larger society. There's no separating the micro (me and my relationship conflicts) from the macro (the clash of civilizations). They interpenetrate. Maybe we've just realized how much religion means to our partner, colleague, or neighbour, and, frankly, we're mystified. The clash of civilizations is taking place between our sheets, work cubicles, and property fences. Like it or not, religion plays a part in our relationship conflicts and in conflict transformation. And, based on current trends, its part in the drama is only going to get bigger.

The twentieth century was marked by violent binary splits: fascism (and Nazism) versus liberal democracies; socialism versus an unrestrained free market. Race conflicts pitted whites against blacks; gender conflicts pitted women against men in politics, work, and personal lives.

Some progress has been made on most of these fronts. Many of us are thinking about these splits in more complex ways. We realize that there are shades of grey, that no one is completely good or bad, that systems have their strengths and weaknesses. That injustice needs confronting, but that real progress takes time. Some battles have been won and we are no longer stuck in code red (limbic-driven) concerning these issues. It's now a matter of putting justice into practice.

Surprisingly, introducing a new religious binary split for the twenty-first century seemed natural to many, while many more were thinking religion was on the wane, its teeth pulled.

Perhaps we prefer having a binary split in our world view, creating one even if it doesn't really exist!

The new binary split in our contemporary world view often pits science against religion, and atheists against religious believers. A simplified version of science (for example, all that is rational, progressive, and effective in our world) is pitted against a simplified version of religion (for example, all that is backward, superstitious, and intolerant in our world). Religion has become the new dividing line, creating the new "us and them" split. A secular world view is pitted against a religious world view. Or it's about *our* religion versus *their* religion. Or it's about moderate religion versus extreme religion. We live in a world of religious violence, fundamentalism, terrorism, 9/11, 7/7. On all these issues, you are either with us or against us, says the Matrix.

In this way, our own IC levels are connected to a larger thinking system. If we want to raise our IC levels, and rattle the bigger cage while we are at it, we need to get hold of how we think about religion. If we don't challenge binary thinking here, the larger world-view system will entice us back to low IC.

Religious conflicts can be the hardest conflict of all
We may be embroiled in a religious conflict right now. The stakes seem high and there is no middle ground. We may be in a violent disagreement with someone who is bolstered by their religious world view. People who do not have a religious world view can feel that those who do are unfairly defended. Certain topics are out of bounds – "That's our faith!" is their response to our questions. We start out feeling threatened even before conflict proceedings with religious people begin. Surely *they* (not us) will be thinking in black and white. We may be married to this person. It gets even harder when both our families disapprove of our religious differences.

Our religious conflict may be with neighbours of a different faith. Perhaps conflict is within our church, synagogue, mosque, or temple. It may be split between theological or personality camps. In the Christian church today, for example, these splits often run along lines of charismatics versus non-charismatics, evangelicals versus liberals, the traditional robed choir versus the happy-clappies.

Religious conflicts can be the hardest conflict of all.[2] In these conflicts, we face the five brain challenges (Chapter 2) and the five social challenges (Chapter 3), along with belief in transcendent and moral absolutes. Tough stuff.

Sheila married Mike, and swiftly discovered that she had also married his family – not just the family members who lived down the road and popped in much more often than she would like, but the family members who lived inside Mike's head. And they were all, to her mind, fundamentalists. There were clear rules for everything. The rules of their married life were set down by the invisible family tribunal in Mike's head. What would Mother say about this? What would Uncle think about that? The problem was she didn't like their taste, their kind of food, their kind of holidays, their kind of music. She hated to admit it, but their different religious backgrounds clashed. This was the great unspoken – the elephant in the room – that nearly every argument circled around, nearly every day.

Hilda's son Toby joined a New Age religious group as soon as he moved to his university digs. It wasn't one of those evil cults in which they all move to the jungle and commit suicide, but it was still some weird sort of new religion, with chanting and ley lines and Stonehenge. Hilda didn't approve of the new Toby; she wanted her real son back. Instead, when he visited, he would talk about how he and his new friends lived on some higher spiritual plane, superior to her way of life. Hilda's blood would boil as her son refused her cooking and would only eat organic, vegan food, and drink herbal teas. He meditated and chanted and had "inner peace", while she sat downstairs and watched television. Hilda and her son could not even sit down for breakfast without some eruption over the wasteful packaging of the breakfast cereal or the amount of sugar she put in her tea.

Underneath these mundane clashes lie different belief systems. Underneath the belief systems rest important values. Some of these values will be non-negotiable, absolutes. You sense that in the other person. They are so stubborn. The temptation is to respond to these conflicts with low IC: "If only you would set yourself free from your family – who incidentally are all religious nutters – we could get on with our own life!"; "If you weren't so brainwashed by those chanting friends of yours who are just sponging your money off you, you could finish your university course. Instead, you are ruining your life with this religious claptrap."

If we respond with low IC, we will be on a downward spiral of black and white duelling. Low IC begets low IC in the other party. It misses out on affirming the deep values of the genuinely religious person. Under threat, religious people will fight back to defend their values. The tendency is for both parties to "absolutize" their viewpoints. This is how we fall into the lap of the new binary. Resist. The limbic system is flying.

As we slow and prime (see Chapter 4), what we need to do is to reach out with a high-IC move. After taking time to reflect on our own viewpoint, we seek to understand the deep values that underlie the religious person's views. For Toby, the underlying value to his spiritual pilgrimage may be his search for a life of meaning and purpose. He may be looking for a way to belong in life. Or he may be looking for a way of getting rid of his former drug-taking, in order to live a life of discipline.

For Sheila's husband Mike, the underlying value to all the strict rules may have to do with family togetherness. The joy of family unity may be the most important value to Mike, and so he doesn't mind taking the opinions of his elders as marching orders. He comes from a close-knit family, and this is core to his spirituality. He feels this is what God wants too. Sheila comes from a more independent family who never talked about religion. Everyone did their own thing. Yet what Sheila most longs for is exactly this – a close-knit family. When Sheila affirmed Mike in his deeply held value of family unity, Mike felt less defensive. He felt that Sheila was coming over to his way of seeing things. He could let down his guard and try to meet Sheila halfway. By agreeing with Sheila on the value of family unity, Mike could see that he also needed to honour Sheila's need for personal integrity. He could see that, as a good husband, he should not pressure her to conform to his family against her own personal integrity. Mike now had the confidence that the deepest value was held in common. The concrete specifics, the religious dos and don'ts, could be talked about without explosions. Eventually, Sheila and Mike came to embrace a wider set of values: not just family unity with its religious underpinnings, but personal integrity and freedom as well. The weaving together of these values for Sheila and Mike might not add up to a simple "both/and". Sheila and Mike may agree that family unity is their highest shared value and that personal integrity nestles under it. They may both feel it is right to support personal integrity as long as family unity is not completely ruptured. Other couples may come to a different solution. Each couple needs to weave together their own high-IC tapestry to affirm their different core values. When a person feels that their deepest values are being respected, their defences come down. The door opens for a mutual search to find creative, non-violent ways of fulfilling those values.

Values, values, values

This is the building block: taking our opponent's deepest values seriously. There are people who would rather die, literally, than renounce their deepest values. This is the non-negotiable when seeking to transform conflict involving religious difference, whether between non-religious and religious people, two religious people, or between religions. Deepest values must be respected. This is not to say there will be agreement on points of doctrine. Now is not the time to finesse the specifics. Unless we are very knowledgable theologians and experts in interfaith dialogue, we are not in a position to question the validity of people's religious beliefs. But we can, as fellow human beings, agree upon shared values. So we build upon what we can agree upon, and these are shared human values including justice, freedom, integrity, compassion, the value of human life, unity, and the search for truth. Admittedly, this approach will not be fruitful with all so-called "belief systems". When Nazism was forcefully crushed at the close of the Second World War, there was nothing convincing left of Nazi ideology. It had been revealed as morally bankrupt, based on lies. There were no values to agree upon.

Religious people may be OK, but I can't stand religion

Even if we can get on with some religious people, some of us still can't stand religion. What is the peculiar threat that religion poses in our largely secular era? Why this new binary in the Matrix? Our guess is that it has something to do with our dread of unequal conflict.

People whom we consider to be *impossible* conflict partners usually have a greater power behind them. They have a system – an organization or ideology that backs them up, that makes them unassailable. We may have experienced religious people using their beliefs as a bolstering system. We expect our religious conflict partners to deploy black and white thinking and only use low levels of IC in order to defend the system that in turn defends them. And we feel that is unfair.

It is true that sometimes religious people do behave this way. So do passionate ideologues of any form: political, social, scientific, cultural. Research shows that people who hold extreme views, whether their views are political, social, or religious, are not very good at perceiving the perspective of the other with whom they disagree. Extreme Right (neo-Nazi), extreme Left (Marxist or Communist), or fervent atheist belief systems (such as the new atheism espoused by Richard Dawkins and others) are usually lower in IC than more moderate positions. Extreme views, by definition, perceive only one point of view: their own. Similarly, extremely liberal Christians may be as low in IC as their despised fundamentalist rivals, especially if you lock them together in the same room.[3]

Even our football team can give a religious-like gloss to our lives, providing meaning, ritual, belonging, and ultimate life concerns. We can be extreme about our football team. People can be extreme about anything. Being extreme has its obvious shortcomings but it also has its uses. It can serve a necessary purpose, at least for a while.

The advantages of seeing in black and white

There are times in history when sharp binary distinctions between right and wrong are needed, and it may be that only religion has enough influence to step up to the plate. There are times when gross injustices need to be confronted, and evil practices or distorted visions of God revoked. Revolutions and religious reformations are such moments:

- the Hebrew scriptures/Old Testament command to revoke the widespread practice of child sacrifice;
- the struggle to get rid of the medieval church's sale of indulgences;
- the nineteenth-century abolition of slavery inspired by evangelical Christians;
- the Civil Rights movement of the 1960s, led by Revd Dr Martin Luther King;
- Latin American protest movements of the 1970s supported by Catholic liberation theologians.

A clear stance had to be taken. Just as the IC of individuals drops in the face of threat to important values, so does the IC of groups. This black and white vision is reflected in the religious writings of such periods. Without this sharp demarcation between right and wrong practices, it is unlikely that the religious leaders of those times would have been able to mobilize people to confront the evils of their day.

Thanks to the moral energies mobilized by black and white preaching, the old wrongs are righted. A cause for celebration. Gradually, life moves on. New challenges emerge. It becomes necessary to rub shoulders with old enemies. Indeed, the religious values of compassion and charity require that the righteous in-group makes peace with the former out-group. The once two-fold, black and white, low-IC religious value system enlarges to embrace a wider array of values[4] – tradition *and* innovation, civil order *and* freedom of belief, equality *and* free enterprise. The wider array of values means the religious world view becomes more complex. It becomes more nuanced as it meets more nuanced circumstances.

In this way, Christianity, Judaism, Islam – indeed, all world religions – can be thought of as naturally complex, naturally high in IC – in the long run. They have all had the task of responding to a host of challenges throughout their histories. IC rises as civilizations become more complex; IC plummets in response to threat. Then IC may recover. Over the long run, the faith encompasses this wide array of IC levels, across a spectrum of low to high IC.

Religion, thus, can be a high-IC force for conflict resolution. Like St Francis, you might wish to pray, hope and work toward being an instrument of peace; and peacemakers such as Archbishop Desmond Tutu in South Africa, Bishop Belo in East Timor, Ricardo Equivera in Columbia, Mairead Corrigan Maguire in Northern Ireland, and others have enabled warring parties to make peace over the crimes of the past. Following their (and other less internationally known examples) a hidden army of faith-based conflict resolution specialists are at work in troubled areas around the world.

Sliding back into black and white

But religious people, just like anyone, can slide back into black and white. Jesus lamented that his generation did not perceive the way of peace he was modelling. In his day, Zealots viewed their situation in first-century Palestine in black and white terms. They were desperate to overthrow the unjust yoke of Roman rule. The Zealots openly revolted. This provoked Roman invasion and the ruin of Jerusalem. Religious faith can inspire high-IC conflict resolution, but it can also return us to low IC when under threat.

Making sense of fundamentalisms

Thousands of studies have been launched since the 1979

Iranian Revolution to try to understand the fundamentalisms blooming in so many corners of the world. Surely, say the secularists, in the modern age, religion should be on its way out. Rather, it appears that religion is fighting back, gaining ground, but sometimes in this peculiar new form.

Among the bewildering array of fundamentalisms, one common thread is apparent. Under a sense of threat, religious belief systems shift from their normally high-IC baseline to become more black and white.[5] The backdrop to this today appears to be the onward rush of globalization. Secular, Western-influenced cultures are rubbing shoulders with traditional cultures in new ways. Through the internet, media, and popular culture, they are invading every nook and cranny. This cultural shift creates a hostile terrain for traditionally religious people. Their values and way of life are being threatened. In this terrain, fundamentalisms, of whatever variety, fight back. Their faith takes a less complex, more black and white shape than the parent religion from which they sprang. This pattern takes many shapes – Islamist extremism, Christian fundamentalists who commit violent acts, Hindu purists.

It must be acknowledged that violence belongs to a tiny, tiny minority of religious activists. However, these activists need a black and white audience before whom to perform their black and white actions. In this light, it seems that fundamentalism is the simplified form religion takes when it is under threat.[6]

Do fundamentalist belief systems bounce back to their original high-IC form once the threat is removed? Not always. The old black and white ways have worked well. The new leadership is loath to let go of its power formed under high-stress conditions. So let's keep the stress conditions alive with continued black and white preaching! It works. And it is so easy to do. Here is the formula: "We are right; you are wrong. You are either with us or against us. There are terrible things that are happening in the world (this part is probably true); only we have the solution to these terrible crimes (this part is not exclusively true)."

And so a belief system forged under conditions of genuine threat to moral values can continue to keep the threat alive, even in easier times. People seem to respond eagerly to a low-IC message if the message matches their current IC levels (lowered through the challenges of recent history, through personal hardship, or through stress induced by hate preaching). Thus preachers of extreme or fundamentalist versions of religion take special care to lower the IC levels of their listeners. It isn't hard to do, because we are all prone to lower our IC whenever a sense of threat is evoked. Then their message makes sense. Under threat, it always makes sense to have an external enemy to blame for our current ills.

A high-IC view of religion

Religious extremism is undoubtedly a problem. But we become part of that problem when we view religious people in low-IC ways. We thereby cement the low-IC dynamic. Yet because religion is inherently complex, there is hope. Even the most black and white fundamentalist belief system has the potential to return to the former high-IC levels of the parent religion – that is, when a wider array of religious values is included and respected. Fundamentalist belief systems tend to emphasize only one value pole – for example, obedience. But the parent religion will also value the opposite pole – personal integrity. Resolution of conflicts with fundamentalists depends on finding a way to weave a wider set of values into a high-IC tapestry.

Fundamentalists are us

We may be high-IC about most areas of life, but we may be low-IC concerning religious issues. This pattern shows up in fundamentalists.[7] It shows up with non-fundamentalist, liberal religious people too. Both have somewhat low IC when it comes to thinking about their out-group (those who take opposing views).[8] We do this as well. We tend to view ourselves as complex thinkers, but we view those who take an opposing world view in more simple, stereotyped ways: "They're all like that." We are a bit "fundamentalist" about fundamentalists. We need to move on from this over-simplification and become open to a higher-IC view concerning the religious tensions of our era, seeing them in all their complexity. If we do not, we are taking up our assigned places on the twenty-first-century map, riven by its religious split. We become part of the Matrix.

Transforming conflict with religious extremists

Humility is the starting point. We have to acknowledge that, in an interaction with someone we view as a religious extremist, we are probably as low-IC as they are.

Next, we aim truly to learn about the other. We aim to see them in all their complexity. This does not mean we agree with them. We may hate their methods (especially violent ones). But if we are not in an emergency situation where life is at stake, now is the time to raise IC and try to understand how this person sees their world. Deploy active listening skills to hear their perspective. Use slow and prime to stay calm and open to what they are saying. (Revisit Chapter 4 to review how to use these tools.) What makes them tick? What are their deepest values? Sometimes we find that those we hate share some values that we too would defend.

We might surprise them. We can help to take down the binary world view of the "other" by ambushing their expectations of us, their out-group. Like the good Samaritan, we help our "enemies" discover friends in places they didn't expect. (See Chapter 3.)

When we understand why others are threatened, what injustices and oppressions they experience in their lives, and why they need a black and white system to defend themselves, we start a mutual journey towards liberation.

Liberation from the binary world view – with the help of friendship
People who are in an oppressed state feel they have no voice of their own. They are dependent on others for giving them shape. Oppressive others may be telling the fused person that they are bad, wicked, stupid, or inferior. The help of a good friend, counsellor, spiritual director, life coach, or mentor is needed; just as Gandhi was needed for India, and Martin Luther King was needed for African Americans. Each one of us needs someone to help us take the first step: to begin to listen to our own perspective: "Who am I? What do I really feel and think?" To listen to this without judgment, with acceptance, is to begin to discover the real self and to affirm our own identity. Gradually we start to realize that we have been hoodwinked into colluding, agreeing with our oppressors.[9]

As we start to see our fused, oppressed state, and the way we have internalized it, we get angry. We won't put up with it any more. Anger gives us a lot of useful energy. We will need it for the uphill struggle ahead. We will face resistance in ourselves and in others as we make changes in the way we live. We need enough anger to give us energy and courage, but not so much that we get out of control.

A good counsellor or soul friend will help to keep us from overreacting in this phase.

As we begin to emerge from a state glued to others, we start to oppose those who seem to be controlling us. We begin to resist how the oppressor defines us. It is in this second stage of the journey that we often need to develop a black and white world view: adolescents against parents, feminists against patriarchal males, workers against fat cats, blacks against whites, true believers against unbelievers, Islamists against those who compromise with corrupt regimes. The black and white world of resistance seems to be a necessary step forward from the fused state. By necessity this world is of low complexity. A fundamentalist belief system will make good sense to us here, and it will provide needed leverage to fight back.

The two-fold-split world view is attractive to us because it mobilizes us. It is a clear-cut world that tells us who is wrong and who is right. It enables us to get out of our paralysed situation. We now know what to do.

Hesitantly, trembling, we draw a line. Rosa Parks refuses to move to the back of the bus, as segregation in the American South demanded. A boundary is set. Whoosh – the reaction reverberates. Somehow, we hold our ground.

There is no going back to the earlier fused consciousness. Fundamentalist religious belief systems are making sense here. Help is needed from beyond ourselves. A sudden conversion may occur. The new-found faith is not a mere crutch; it enables us to begin to stand on our own two feet. It helps to define what to resist. It gives the moral courage to take a stand. It identifies real wrongs. It enables us to lever ourselves away from controlling persons. We have God on our side.

We might become locked in this lowered complexity, this black and white way of seeing the world. This invites conflict, as both parties to a dispute tend to match each other's level of complexity. If one side moves to low IC, so does the other.

But it is also possible that the religious person will move on from the low-IC cycle of conflict and revenge. The religion also provides profound resources to support forgiveness, reconciliation, and peacemaking. If the other side responds with higher IC, peacemaking becomes possible. Real grievances need to be addressed. Perceptions of the "other" also need to be addressed. Both oppressors and oppressed probably view themselves as acting in self-defence:

> Oppressor: You are dangerous to me so I will keep you in your box.

> Oppressed: You are harming me so I will fight back. I will put *you* into your box.

Neither side is totally good or totally bad. But both are locked in a spiral of mutual harm. When people move towards higher IC, they begin to see themselves and others in more complex ways. Through mediation and dialogue, both parties can find creative ways to weave together opposing perspectives. Some win–win solutions may emerge, and a shared identity as fellow human beings may become possible.

Emergencies will still happen

The forward thrust of human growth does seem to be towards complexity, and religion can support that forward thrust. There are emergency times when black and white moral decisions are required, and religion supports this too. We see this in the biblical record, as well as in recent history. Religion provides the black and white stance to face down evil. When the emergency is over, religion can provide the resources for forgiveness and reconciliation.

A religious world view becomes high-IC over time, cumulatively. The former ability to see the world in black and white is not erased. Indeed, sometimes high-IC reasoning suffers from too much information, too many peripheral details, making it unclear who is responsible, or what do to.[10] We need low-IC thinking when we have to make stark choices. Nor does religion erase the times of fusion when we felt the security of being "glued" to others. That too remains part of us. The danger about going back is that we may stay there permanently. By resisting the unknown, we may *feel* safe, but when we remain in the black and white emergency state, we are unable to resolve conflict. And eventually this becomes dangerous. We are brewing tomorrow's irresolvable conflicts.

The good news is that we have on our side the natural tendency of human beings to move from simplicity to complexity, to mature from fusion with others toward being connected and separate. We also have on our side the rich and complex religious traditions that do have some high-IC resources. Religion can help move us forward; it doesn't only move us back. Whether we have always been a person of faith, or whether we have had a dramatic conversion, how we understand our beliefs will increase in complexity and unfold as we mature. Those of us who are not religious can grow toward a high-IC view of those who are.

The end is in the beginning
The cycle starts again. From fusion, to black and white, to complex, and back again, for a while. This seems to be a

human and spiritual dynamic, like breathing. We are inwardly urged to press forward to liberation, and then we are pulled back to fused or black and white ways of thinking.

We have to engage with this dynamic cycle. Expanding and contracting, yet moving forward, inch by inch. Moving forward doesn't mean we completely ditch the former ways of fusion or black and white thinking. We need those for emergency situations. This means that our religious, spiritual life cannot, need not, be perfect. We cannot reach some imagined nirvana of perfect high IC. In any case, high IC is impossible to legislate. High IC has to be a voluntary journey. If it were otherwise, it would cease to be liberating.

Religion, which deals with the ultimate concerns and threats to human existence, has this dual nature. When moral danger threatens, we *will* return to the low-IC default state of the brain (the limbic system code red, the social reactions to conflict in full swing). When the odds are stacked against us, often it is religion alone that has the power to be the shaper of shapers – to help us to break away from oppression and to reform the Matrix.

Questions to think about:

1. How would you describe the religious people you know? Do they have high IC? Or low IC?
2. Has this influenced your views of religion more generally?
3. If you have a faith, would you agree with the following statement? "There are black and white aspects to my faith, and there are more inclusive, complex aspects within my faith."

Which beliefs are cast in black and white? What aspects of your faith are "inclusive of the stranger" – for example, more complex than simple "us and them" distinctions (and thus do not easily fit into low-IC black and white terms)?

4. If you are a person of faith, draw a time line of your own approach to your faith. Did it start out complex and become more simple over time, or did it start simple and become more complex over time? It may move up or down according to your life circumstances.

Are there any points where your faith IC level plummets in response to threat or stress? (Plummeting IC levels could take the form of defending beliefs in a black and white way, or ditching beliefs as "total rubbish". A higher IC approach may more easily tolerate disappointment, paradox, exceptions to the rule.)

5. If you are not a person of faith, would you say your views of religion allow for disagreement or require others to agree with you? Draw a time line of how your views of religion developed. Respond to the same questions as in number 4 regarding complex to simple or simple to complex and plummeting IC levels.

High IC, complex

Low IC, simple

Time

CHAPTER 8

A guide to being an agent for peace: I can do it

Although conflict continues to erupt around the globe, what has changed significantly since 1945 is the huge number of conflicts ending and how swiftly they are ending.[1] This is a new turn in history. It's not just that UN and NATO peacekeeping interventions are always successful. Many times they are not. But along with those needed efforts come an army of peacemaking individuals and NGOs (non-governmental organizations) working on the ground, resolving conflict between individuals, villages, and national areas. And this is what is making the difference. Peace cannot be imposed; it has to be generated from the ground up, by ordinary people. By us.

A. Principles of peacekeeping

We are in charge. We will not be pushed around by our brain, our emotions, other people, our conflict partner, our upbringing, or the Matrix. Peacekeeping and peacemaking is first person "I". We choose to make the conflict situation safe for ourselves and others.

1. Be safe

At a time when you and your potential conflict partners are not in a live conflict – a time in which you're both relaxed – discuss and agree to the rules of conflict. Describe the behaviours that are to be considered out of bounds in any future conflict. Consider the whole range of possible behaviours: physical or sexual violence, verbal violence that vilifies, demeans, or shames. One or both parties walking out, refusing to engage in efforts to resolve conflict, might also be an unacceptable behaviour.

Drink, drugs, and conflict are a lethal combination. All of your top-level thinking and relational skills need to be in good working order to deal with conflict. You need all of your neocortex for the task. Agree to come back to it when you both are sober. Walk away if those lines are crossed. Agree to return when the boundaries can be kept.

If violence of any kind, drugs, or alcohol have been a feature of your arguments, start out with a relationship counsellor before working with IC. Safety needs to be established, and a skilled third party (counsellor) can ensure that.

Safety comes first, and then move towards identifying comfort zones. The idea is that both parties need to feel comfortable with the proceedings. Agree on what are permissible expressions of anger. For example, showing anger with raised voices or even slamming doors may be acceptable, but not shaking a fist in the other person's face or throwing things. Different people have different thresholds, perhaps not wanting raised voices, or wanting verbal exchanges kept "polite" in specific ways. Defer to the one who feels uncomfortable with something so that both parties feel comfortable enough to participate.

2. *Maintenance*
Don't wait until a conflict erupts to figure out interpersonal differences. Use the self-discovery quizzes and Big 5 lenses separately and then discuss them together, ahead of an actual conflict. Practice active listening skills so that they become like a good pair of running shoes, easy to slip into when needed for running the distance during conflict. Discuss the conflict levels and act now to build trust and improve communication. Challenge one another to use IC in low-stress situations, branching as much as possible for five minutes and then weaving as much as possible for ten minutes, and comparing notes. Familiarize yourself with your armoury and use it to deepen the peace in your relationships.

3. *Tune-ups*
Care for your body. It is the first place to register a broken peace. Feed your brain and body (refer back to the slow and prime strategies), exercise, rest, relax. Practise slow, deep breathing. Keep your whole self primed for peacekeeping and you'll be ready for peacemaking.

B. Peacemaking
This map is an "easy guide". If you need to review the nitty-gritty detail, then return to Chapter 4 and revisit the *A to Z of IC: Getting from 1 to 7*.

1. *Keep safe*
Stick to previous agreements on what is allowed when

showing anger and the other rules of combat. Remember the five brain challenges: your limbic system will try to goad you into thinking that you are unsafe. Remind yourself that conflict is difficult and painful, but you will not die. Deep inhale, slow exhale. Use the slow and prime steps.

Try holding hands or having some other non-demanding physical contact at some point to remind yourselves of your bond. You value the bond, even though you are angry. This helps both people to feel safe and in the relationship.

By entering into this conflict consciously, you signal that you agree to close your exits (not flee from the relationship even though it has conflict) and to keep working at the conflict until there is some resolve. Even if you have to walk away temporarily because you are getting out of control, you agree to return to it.[2]

2. Know and hang on to your own perspective

In the face of threat, our own perspective can collapse or harden into a point-by-point memorandum. Either way, use the self-discovery tools and listening strategies to get in touch with all of your feelings.

If you know your own viewpoint in detail, then sit with it and get beneath it. What are you longing for? What really matters to you in this conflict?

If you don't know your perspective, what are you feeling? Angry, stressed, scared, disappointed, or sad? Use an internet search engine to find names of emotions with accompanying faces (try typing in: "feeling face cards" and you'll see many examples on the sites that come up). Notice which faces make you say, "Yeah, that's it. That's how I feel."

Once you have dug beneath your feelings to your deeper longings, then start talking to yourself. That's right.

Start speaking out how you feel in an empty room, perhaps to an empty chair. To get to know your viewpoint well, you need to practise saying it aloud. Verbalizing our feelings actually connects the different sides and layers of our brains; it physiologically activates the connecting neurological pathways.[3] Maybe you need to write it down first and then read it out. Write a letter that you may or may not send. Read it aloud. Talk to a safe person – a wise, trusted friend. Find a spiritual director, counsellor, mentor, or life coach.

In all these methods, you are looking for your deepest values and needs. These are valid. They need to be stated aloud.

Your feelings will build up inside you until you take the time to verbalize (responsibly) your position (abiding by the rules). Eventually you'll explode or implode. You need to speak them out, first to yourself, perhaps to someone else, but eventually to your conflict partner.

When you are confident in knowing your own perspective (and the deep needs and values your position represents), make a date to talk. A well-planned meeting over a disagreement can fail because the timing is wrong. Blood sugar is often low at the end of the day. You don't have enough fuel for the neocortex, so the limbic system gains the upper hand, promoting a black and white view of things. This is not going to help. Make a date when you both are sufficiently rested and refreshed to be able to rise to conflict transformation.

Communication in the trenches

i) "I" not "YOU"
Take responsibility for your own perspective by speaking in

first person "I": "I am angry when... I feel hurt if you..." If you've found a counsellor, they will have helped you with this. Ask a friend to help you practise speaking in the first person.

ii) Negatives get special handling

If you are bringing up an area of constant irritation, an area in which you constantly find yourself criticizing your partner, recast the wording. Your conflict partner no longer hears what you are saying. Instead of expressing it in the negative, re-frame it positively as a request.

(a) Take a chronic complaint: "You never listen to me when we talk over dinner."

(b) Isolate the desire: "I really want to feel like we're each sharing our days and what's going on in our lives."

(c) List the target activities: "Let's take turns over dinner on Mondays, Wednesdays, and Fridays talking about what's going on in our days so we can celebrate good things and help with challenges. Other nights we can just relax, talk about current events, share family and friend updates, or watch the news."[4]

Marriages need to maintain a ratio of 9:1 positive to negative experiences, in order to keep the marriage healthy. We don't avoid the negative. We state it responsibly (in first person "I"), carefully (with caveats such as "You probably didn't mean to, but I felt humiliated when you said that"), and surrounded with positive things that can be said truthfully ("I love you and want our relationship to work", "It's great going out with you and relaxing with your friends from work", "I feel as if I get a glimpse of your working life", plus four more positive statements... "But I really suffer when you criticize me in public"). The target behaviours that you want changed are made clear and concrete. ("Next time we go out with your friends from work, please do not tease me about my weight or my failed diets in front of them. Just don't mention it. Talk about something else.")

In this way, the positive operates like a container for the negative. The negative is explosive and needs careful handling. The positive motivates you to transform the negative safely, detonating it in order to build rather than destroy. If you think your relationship is in a weak state, take special care. You can not drive a ten-ton truck over a two-ton bridge. You need to unload the truck and only take what is absolutely essential over the fragile bridge. Use all the self-discovery tools to identify what is absolutely essential to address in this relationship.

NOT: "I hate being with you and your friends. All you do is gripe and cut people down, including me."

RATHER: "I appreciate that your friends are really important to you, that you need to have fun with them after the pressures of work, and it's nice to be included, but please find another topic of conversation other than my weight."

NOT: "I hate being with your family every Christmas. Every year it's the same old thing. When do I get to have something for me?"

RATHER: "When we spend all our holidays with your parents at the cottage, it makes me feel like I'm not looking after my parents because I'm always with your parents and not mine. Can we find a way to share this out more equally?"

iii) Speak so others can hear
You may feel you are playing a fake role when you reword in this polite way. When you make a date to deliver it, well

rehearsed, you may feel a bit false. You haven't really said it like it is! Your usual gusto and verve is missing; you've not been spontaneous. With practice, it may become more spontaneous to communicate in this new way. It's not false, it's just different. You are practising good communication skills, taking into account how your audience hears. If you were preparing a presentation for work, you'd take as much time. Aren't your close relationships as important? Yes, but are close relationships supposed to involve so much work? It depends what you mean by "work". Effort? Intentionality? Consideration? Yes. Yes. Yes.

Spontaneity may have deteriorated into sabotage. You want to get across your message to your loved one. You can skewer them, but don't expect any change afterwards. (And watch for a skewer to come flying back at you.) In order for the message to be delivered, you have to repackage it so they can receive it. The most important thing is to convey your message, your perspective about the conflict. So, you need to be willing to adapt your usual style (upfront, "in your face"?) for the sake of getting your message communicated. Sometimes familiarity breeds bad communication habits. Your conflict is giving you an opportunity to get rid of them.

Even though you have adopted a more careful style of communication, you will have been true to your own perspective. After delivery, you feel like a 3-D person: "This is who I am. I exist. This is me. And I've said it in a way the other person could hear." This is worth celebrating.

3. Now listen to the other's perspective

i) Listen

While you use your active listening skills, your partner now gets to have their say. What they have to say might be totally in opposition to your viewpoint. This is OK. Just as you are committed to your perspective, you need to allow the other person the right to express their own perspective.

Here is the hard part. Do not interrupt, correct, defend, or try to fix them. Let them have their say. (Quick clarifying questions are OK, as long as they're not veiled corrections.)

You may need to use the slow and prime steps as you listen to the other, because this is really hard to do without getting defensive. What they are saying may well be threatening or anger-making to you.

Like St Francis, you might want to pray, hope and work toward being an instrument of peace: "May I seek not so much to be understood, as to understand." Mirroring back what the other person is saying, even if you totally disagree with it, creates space for them, just as you needed space. Validating what they are saying (letting them know you understand what they are saying) and empathizing (imagining how they are feeling) protects that space and shows respect, even if you still totally disagree. Again, this is what you have wanted for yourself.

Once your conflict partner feels heard, they will feel less threatened. If they have got some of their facts wrong, you can make those factual corrections after you have heard them. ("OK, I hear what you are saying, that you just need to blow off steam after work because your boss is so critical. So you need to have fun with your friends. But you said to your friends that I was always trying to lose weight and never succeeded, and that's not strictly true. I have lost some weight this year.")

When you really hear the other person you no longer see them as the enemy, as all bad, all unreasonable. You see them as 3-D, with some valid points, real needs, and deep values. You may not agree with them, but they are uniquely who they are. They exist.

You still hang on to your perspective as you take this on board. You may remain in total disagreement with one another. Leave it as is. Don't immediately try to get the other person to agree with you. Agree to disagree for now. Use the slow and prime steps. Breathe deeply. Take some time apart. Walk around the block slowly. Look at your visual reminders.

ii) Dig deeper

You may find that you are beginning to see that your own point of view does not mop up all of reality. You remain committed to your own viewpoint and your underlying values, still... "He does have a point." Some of what the other says has validity. Start to dig down to deepest values. What is each of you seeking to protect?

Use the self-discovery quizzes and Big 5 lenses to identify the interpersonal differences as represented by perceptual and conflict styles. What is not really central to the disagreement but is more a matter of focusing on different aspects of the situation?

iii) Connect

This is the magic turning point. The reality of the other person more effectively relativizes your ego than anything else. Your perspective is not the only perspective in the universe. Although it relativizes you, it does not destroy you or invalidate you. You exist; so does the other person. You can both be 3-D, different people in this relationship who see the uniqueness and value of the other. This coexistence enhances and grows each of you. You still do not have to agree.

iv) Expect bumps

If one of you blows up in the course of this process, it's not over. Don't expect perfection from either yourself or the other person. Admit that you got out of control, and agree to come back to it after you both have cooled down. It's OK. Feelings of threat, closing down to low IC, and binary thinking are impersonal. It's no one's fault. It's how the brain functions. Over the course of human history, our brains have learned to function this way. It has helped us to survive in more primitive conditions. But now we are living in different circumstances. The five brain and five social challenges can take us on a disastrous turn, but we can outsmart – and change – our normal brain functioning. We can work through our feelings of being under threat. We can talk ourselves down from the ledge. This takes practice. We can begin again… and again.

Remember, you have both decided to close your exits and to work through the conflict in the context of a committed relationship. Come back in ten minutes. Or next week. Make a date to resume.

4. Weave your way forward

You may need time out again. Change the way you think by changing your physical state. Change your brain by changing your body. Take a walk. Take a bath. Take a power nap. Let the different perspectives simmer and start to integrate.

Try to imagine in your mind's eye what you want to work toward.

Keep in mind each other's deepest needs and values. These may be the non-negotiables. These will need to be honoured in the integration. Aim for win–win. Try doing figure–ground reversals. Try creating unlikely partnerships.

At a prearranged time, come back together to discuss a list of possible integrations/weavings. There may be more than one acceptable way forward.

Having done all this, you may still hit a brick wall. You've tried, you have used the tools, you have worked through the steps and strategies, you have practised beforehand, you have journalled, talked with friends, had counselling, been polite, closed your exits, not driven a ten-ton truck over a two-ton bridge, lovingly packed negatives in positive packaging, and it has still all collapsed.

The conflict is not solved. All that effort, and the other person still does not listen.

You need to explore whether your conflict partner is a difficult person (Chapter 5). If so, what reasonable expectations should you have of high-IC conflict transformation?

We can only change ourselves. We cannot change another person at all. Ever. So you can experience transformation by using all the tools, skills, and strategies to raise your own IC, and this will improve the relationship, but it will never be what it could be if the other person had also raised their own IC.

It may be that this is a conflict that is a truly irresolvable clash of paradigms. We have to agree to disagree. A larger paradigm may result ultimately. Revisit the context of the conflict. Is there a clue there? Revisit the proposed ways forward, even the ones that seemed silly. Do they have anything in common, or is there a connection among them that might point to another way forward? Some of the thorniest disagreements in history have taken the longest to work out, but the ultimate solution was worth the wait. In science, the classic example involves the debate about the nature of light: is it wave-like or particle-like? After many years of debate and disagreement, it turned out that light is both, but it depends on which instrument you use to observe it (the context).[5] Your disagreement might be similar: it might depend on some as yet unrecognized influence. Keep leaning into the opposing viewpoints. Or it might involve something as mysterious as human beings who are both limited and yet capable of transcendence. If you both keep an open mind and heart, you might see something of each in yourselves.

In a sense, Boot Camp never really ends. And yet we do amaze ourselves sometimes. In the midst of conflict we begin to see ourselves behaving much differently from how we have in the past. We listen instead of running away. We present our viewpoint in a way that others can hear – and they do. We recognize our own stress and anxiety signals, taking care before exploding or imploding. We separate interpersonal differences from the actual issues. We become more 3-D. Our conflict partners become more 3-D, in surprising and interesting ways.

We still have setbacks, we still make mistakes, but we are no longer sitting on the edge of disaster. Conflict no longer spells ruin. We see transformation in ourselves and our relationships. We even see some ripples of change in our larger communities. The air around us is charged with possibility. Boot Camp doesn't exactly become a luxury spa, but it engenders a whole new state of mind – one that is hopeful, energizing, and, dare we say it, fun.

Notes

Part One
Introduction

1. Suedfeld, P., Guttieri, K., and Tetlock, P. E., "Assessing integrative complexity at a distance: Archival analyses of thinking and decision making" (pp. 246–72); Suedfeld, P. and Tetlock, P. E., "President Clinton: Cognitive manager in trouble" (pp. 328–32); Suedfeld, P., "Saddam Hussein's integrative complexity under stress" (pp. 391–96); in J. M. Post (Ed.), *The Psychological Assessment of Political Leaders: With Profiles of Saddam Hussein and Bill Clinton*, Ann Arbor: The University of Michigan Press, 2003.

2. Published as Boyd-MacMillan, E. and Savage, S., *Conflict Transformation: Conflict Transformation amongst Senior Church Leaders with Different Theological Stances*, York: FCL Press, 2008.

3. COSCA is the Scottish professional accrediting body for counsellors and therapists.

4. Johnson, B., *Polarity Management: Identifying and Managing Unsolvable Problems*, Amherst, Massachusetts: Human Resource Development Press, 1992; Martin, R., *The Opposable Mind: How Successful Leaders Win through Integrative Thinking*, Boston, Massachusetts: Harvard Business Press, 2009.

5. See Loder, J., *The Transforming Moment*, second edition, Colorado Springs: Helmers & Howard, 1989. Loder traces a fundamental "logic" or "grammar" of transformation at work in all human development, and as examples traces the "logic" at work in therapeutic insights, creative work, and scientific discoveries.

6. For example, Daloz, L. A., *Mentor: Guiding the Journey of Adult Learners*, San Francisco: Jossey-Bass Publishers, 1999.

7. Johnson, B., *Polarity Management: Identifying and Managing Unsolvable Problems*, Amherst, Massachusetts: Human Resource Development Press, 1992.

8. Martin, R., *The Opposable Mind: How Successful Leaders Win through*

Integrative Thinking, Boston, Massachusetts: Harvard Business Press, 2009.

9. Boyd-MacMillan, E., *Transformation: James Loder, Mystical Spirituality, and James Hillman*, Oxford: Peter Lang, AG, 2006. Deep transforming engagement with God does not circumvent but harnesses normal human processes of learning and knowing, and conflict is at the core. See also Boyd-MacMillan, E., "More than collaboration", in *The Way*, vol. 43, no. 4, 2004, pp. 29–40.

10. For example, Meyers, J., *Conflict Free Living: How to Build Healthy Relationships for Life*, (formerly *Life Without Strife*, 1995, 2000), Peabody, Massachusetts: Charisma House, 2008. Joyce Meyers is a *New York Times* best-selling author.

Chapter 1

1. See Loder, J., *The Transforming Moment*, second edition, Colorado Springs: Helmers & Howard, 1989. Loder traces a fundamental "logic" or "grammar" of transformation at work in all human development, and as examples traces the "logic" at work in therapeutic insights, creative work, and scientific discoveries.
Daloz, L. A., *Mentor: Guiding the Journey of Adult Learners*, San Francisco: Jossey-Bass Publishers, 1999. Daloz encourages mentors to facilitate the provocation of conflicts to develop thinking in students.
Johnson, B., *Polarity Management: Identifying and Managing Unsolvable Problems*, Amherst, Massachusetts: Human Resource Development Press, 1992. Johnson identifies conflicts between opposing points of view as core to business and personnel development.
Martin, R., *The Opposable Mind: How Successful Leaders Win through Integrative Thinking*, Boston, Massachusetts: Harvard Business Press, 2009. Martin identifies the ability to manage opposing points of view as key to business management.

2. For example, see Boyd-MacMillan, E. and Savage, S., *Transforming Conflict: Conflict Transformation amongst Senior Church Leaders with Different Theological Stances*, York: FCL Press, 2008; and Savage, S. and Boyd-MacMillan, E., *The Human Face of Church: A Social Psychology and Pastoral Theology Resource for Pioneer and Traditional Ministry*, London: SCM Press, 2007.

3. Suedfeld, P., Guttieri, K. and Tetlock, P. E., "Assessing integrative complexity at a distance: Archival analyses of thinking and decision making" (pp. 246–72); Suedfeld, P. and Tetlock, P. E., "President Clinton: Cognitive manager in trouble" (pp. 328–32); Suedfeld, P., "Saddam Hussein's integrative complexity under stress" (pp. 391–96); in J. M. Post (Ed.), *The Psychological Assessment of Political Leaders: With*

Profiles of Saddam Hussein and Bill Clinton, Ann Arbor: The University of Michigan Press, 2003.

4. "Differentiation" is the technical term for what we are calling "branching out", or "branching" for short. It refers to the recognition of new information, many alternatives, and nuances. See Baker-Brown, G., Ballard, E. J., Bluck, S., de Vries, B., Suedfeld, P., and Tetlock, P. E., *Coding Manual for Conceptual/Integrative Complexity*, University of British Columbia and University of California (Berkeley), 1992.

5. "Integration" is the technical term for what we are calling "weaving together", or "weaving" for short. It refers to the recognition of relationships among differences and an ability to view them in combinatorial ways. See Baker-Brown, G., Ballard, E. J., Bluck, S., de Vries, B., Suedfeld, P., and Tetlock, P. E., *Coding Manual for Conceptual/Integrative Complexity*, University of British Columbia and University of California (Berkeley), 1992.

6. Suedfeld, P. and Rank, A. D., "Revolutionary leaders: Long-term success as a function of changes in conceptual complexity" in *Journal of Personality and Social Psychology*, 34, 1976, pp. 169–78; Suedfeld, P. and Tetlock, P. E., "Integrative complexity of communications in international crises" in *Journal of Conflict Resolution*, 21, 1977, pp. 169–84; Suedfeld, P. and Wallace, M. D., "President Clinton as a cognitive manager" (pp. 215–33) in S. A. Renshon (Ed.), *The Clinton Presidency*, Oxford: Westview Press, 1995; Suedfeld, P. and Walbaum, A. B. C., "Altering integrative complexity in political thought: Value conflict and audience agreement" in *InterAmerican Journal of Psychology*, 26, 1992, pp. 19–36; Suedfeld, P., Leighton, D. C., and Conway, L. G. III, "Integrative Complexity and Cognitive Agreement in International Confrontations: Research and Potential Applications" in M. Fitzduff and C. E. Stout (Eds.), *The Psychology of Resolving Global Conflicts: From War to Peace*, vol. 1, New York: Praeger, 2006, pp. 211–37.

7. Levine, P., *Healing Trauma: A Pioneering Program for Restoring the Wisdom of Your Body*, Boulder, Colorado: Sounds True Inc., 2005. See also Levine, P., *Waking the Tiger – Healing the Trauma: The Innate Capacity to Transform Overwhelming Experiences*, Berkeley, California: North Atlantic Books, 1997.

8. See Robinson, M., *Peace Between the Sheets*, Berkeley, California: Frog Books (imprint of North Atlantic Books Inc.), 2003; *Cupid's Poisoned Arrow: From Habit to Harmony in Sexual Relationships*, Berkeley, California: North Atlantic Books Inc., 2009; and website www.reuniting.info. Thanks to Mary Sharpe for introducing us to this research.

9. These approaches to relationship draw on two psychological theories called "social exchange theory" and "equity theory". See Kelley, H. H. and Thibaut, J. W., *Interpersonal Relations: A Theory of Interdependence*, Chichester: Wiley, 1978; Clark, M. S. and Mills, J., "Interpersonal Attraction in Exchange and Communal Relationships" in *Journal of Personality and Social Psychology*, vol. 37, 1979, pp. 12–24; and Vangelisti, A. and Perlman, D. *The Cambridge Handbook of Personal Relationships*, Cambridge, UK: Cambridge University Press, 2006.

10. Hendrix, H., *Getting the Love You Want*, London: Simon & Shuster, 1993.

11. Hendrix, H., *Getting the Love You Want*, London: Simon & Shuster, 1993. Hendrix insists on this decision from each partner for the duration of the couple's therapy.

12. Archer, J. 'Sex differences in aggression between heterosexual partners: A meta-anayltic review' in *Psychological Bulletin*, 126, 651–680, 2000.

Chapter 2

1. Levine, P., *Waking the Tiger – Healing the Trauma: The Innate Capacity to Transform Overwhelming Experiences*, Berkeley, California: North Atlantic Books, 1997.

2. See MacLean, P., *The Triune Brain in Evolution: Bibliographical Excerpts*, New York: Plenum Press, 1990. Although the mechanics of MacLean's theory are questioned, there is good evidence to support the triune structure.

3. LeDoux, J. E., *The Emotional Brain: The Mysterious Underpinnings of Emotional Life*, New York: Simon & Schuster, 1996.

4. Levine, P., *Healing Trauma: A Pioneering Program for Restoring the Wisdom of Your Body*, Boulder, Colorado: Sounds True, 2005, 2008; Levine, P., *Waking the Tiger – Healing the Trauma: The Innate Capacity to Transform Overwhelming Experiences*, Berkeley, California: North Atlantic Books, 1997.

5. Allport, G., *The Nature of Prejudice*, Reading, Massachusetts: Addison-Wesley, 1954; Tajfel, H., *Human Groups and Social Categories*, Cambridge, UK: Cambridge University Press, 1981.

6. Screened in the UK on Sunday 5 April 2009. Written by Guy Hibbert.

7. For example, Sam Wollaston, "Sam Wollaston on the weekend's TV" in The *Guardian*, 6 April 2009.

8. Hendrix, H., *Getting the Love You Want*, London: Simon & Shuster, 1993.

9. Kruglanski, A., *The Psychology of Closed-Mindedness: Essays in Social Psychology*, New York, NY: Psychology Press, 2004.

10. Based on the novel series of the same name by Robert Ludlum.

11. Based on the novel series of the same name by J. R. R. Tolkien.

12. Herman, J., *Trauma and Recovery: The Aftermath of Violence – From Domestic Abuse to Political Terror*, New York: Basic Books, 1997; Levine, P. *Waking the Tiger – Healing the Trauma: The Innate Capacity to Transform Overwhelming Experiences*, Berkeley, California: North Atlantic Books, 1997.

13. Levine, P., *Healing Trauma: A Pioneering Programme for Restoring the Wisdom of Your Body*, Boulder, Colorado: Sounds True, Inc., 2009, p. 9.

14. Cairns, K., *Attachment, Trauma and Resilience: Therapeutic Caring for Children*, British Association for Adoption and Fostering, 2002.

15. Volf, M., *Exclusion and Embrace: A Theological Exploration of Identity, Otherness, and Reconciliation*, Nashville: Abingdon Press, 1996.

16. See McIntosh, A., *Hell and High Water: Climate Change, Hope and the Human Condition*, Edinburgh: Birlinn Limited, 2008.

17. Savage, S., "Toward Integrative Solutions to Moral Disputes Between Conservative and Liberal Christians" in *Journal of Psychology and Christianity*, special issue on forgiveness, 2008.

18. Boyd-MacMillan, E. and Savage, S., *Transforming Conflict: Conflict Transformation Amongst Senior Church Leaders with Different Theological Stances*, York: FCL Press, 2008.

19. Watts, F., Nye, R., and Savage, S., *Psychology for Christian Ministry*, London: Routledge, 2008, p. 18; Whitehouse, H., *Modes of Religiosity: A Cognitive Theory of Religious Transmission*, Australia: James Bennett Pty Ltd, 2004.

20. The popular books of John Gray (for example, *Men are from Mars, Women are from Venus*) have reinforced this view.

21. Gray, J., *Men are from Mars, Women are from Venus: A Practical Guide for Improving Communication and Getting What You Want in Your Relationships*, Thorsons, 1993.

22. See Cameron, D., *The Myth of Mars and Venus: Do Men and Women Really Speak Different Languages?*, Oxford: Oxford University Press, 2007; and "A Language in Common" in *The Psychologist*, vol. 22, no. 7, 2009, pp. 578–80.

23. Van Leeuwen, M. S., Eastern University, BACIP, Third Keynote Lecture, "Men are from Earth, Women are from Earth: The Psychology of Gender since C. S. Lewis", April 2008, pp. 5–6.

24. See Savage, S. and Boyd-MacMillan, E., *The Human Face of*

Church: A Social Psychology and Pastoral Theology Resources for Pioneer and Traditional Ministry, London: SCM Press, 2007, Chapter 3: "No Conflict Here, We're All Christians!" for some of the challenges particular to conflict in faith communities.

25. Parkin, A., *Explorations in Cognitive Neuropsychology*, Hove, UK: Psychology Press, 1996, see chapter on "Split Brain"; see also Taylor, J., *My Stroke of Insight: A Brain Scientist's Personal Journey*, New York: Plume Books (Penguin), 2009.

26. Rapp, B., *The Handbook of Neuropsychology: What Deficits Reveal About the Human Mind*, Hove, UK: Psychology Press, 2000.

27. De Dreu, C. K. W. and van Knippenberg, D., "The Possessive Self as a Barrier to Conflict Resolution: Effects of Mere Ownership, Process Accountability, and Self-Concept Clarity on Competitive Cognitions and Behaviour" in *Journal of Personality and Social Psychology*, vol. 89, no. 3, 2005, pp. 345–57.

Chapter 3

1. "Villa fans, violence and me" in *The Guardian: Foul Play, The Seven Deadly Sins of Football*, 18 May 2009, p. 7.

2. For more information visit www.mr-squirrel.co.uk.

3. Hendrix, H., "The Evolution of Imago Relationship Therapy: A Personal and Professional Journey" in H. Hendrix, H. Hunt, M. Hannah, and W. Luquet (Eds.), *Imago Relationship Theory: Perspectives on Theory*, San Francisco: Jossey-Bass, a Wiley Imprint, 2005, pp. 32–33.

4. Plumlee, S. R., "Relationship Knowing: Imago and Object Relations" in H. Hendrix, H. Hunt, M. Hannah, and W. Luquet (Eds.), *Imago Relationship Theory: Perspectives on Theory*, San Francisco: Jossey-Bass, a Wiley Imprint, 2005, p. 119.

5. Tajfel, H., Flament, C., Billig, M. G., and Bundy, R. P., "Social Categorization and Intergroup Behaviour" in *European Journal of Social Psychology*, 1, 1971, pp. 149–78; Tajfel, H., "Social Psychology of Intergroup Relations" in *Annual Review of Psychology*, 33, 1982, pp. 1–30; Brewer, M. B., "In-group Bias in the Minimal Intergroup Situation: A Cognitive-motivational Analysis" in *Psychological Bulletin*, 86, 1979, pp. 307–24. For more on in-group and out-group behaviour in faith communities, see Savage, S. and Boyd-MacMillan, E., *The Human Face of Church: A Social Psychology and Pastoral Theology Resource for Pioneer and Traditional Ministry*, London: SCM Press, 2007, Chapter 1: "The Human Side of Church: Group Processes in Congregations".

6. Luke 10:29–36 from *The Message* version of the Bible, a paraphrase

by pastor and biblical languages scholar, Eugene Peterson.

7. Sayle, A., "The writing was on the wall" in *The Sunday Times Magazine*, 3 May 2009, p. 9.

8. See Gerhardt, S., *Why Love Matters: How Affection Shapes a Baby's Brain*, London: Routledge, 2004. This book draws together a huge amount of research and presents it very accessibly. The connections between physiological development, emotional capacities, and early life experiences will both amaze and terrify, but it's never too late to expand our emotional and relational capacities.

9. Koltko-Rivera, M. E., "The Psychology of World views" in *Review of General Psychology*, vol. 8, no. 1, 2004, pp. 3–58.

10. Koltko-Rivera, M. E., "The Psychology of World views" in *Review of General Psychology*, vol. 8, no. 1, 2004, pp. 3–58.

11. These questions are original to Middleton, J. R. and Walsh, B. J., *Truth is Stranger Than It Used to Be: Biblical Faith in a Postmodern Age*, London: SPCK, 1995. The questions first appeared in Middleton and Walsh's earlier book, *The Transforming Vision: Shaping a Christian World view*, Downers Grove, Illinois: Inter-Varsity Press, 1984. N. T. Wright uses these questions in his book *The New Testament and the People of God: Christian Origins and the Question of God*, London: SPCK, 1992, p. 124, adding a fifth question, "What time is it?"

12. Allport, G., *The Nature of Prejudice*, Reading, Massachusetts: Addison-Wesley, 1954; Tajfel, H., *Human Groups and Social Categories*, Cambridge, UK: Cambridge University Press, 1981.

Chapter 4

1. See Baker-Brown, G., Ballard, E. J., Bluck, S., de Vries, B., Suedfeld P., and Tetlock, P. E., *Coding Manual for Conceptual/Integrative Complexity*, University of British Columbia and University of California (Berkeley), 1992.

2. Cyhlarora, E., Bell, J. G., Dick, J. R., Mackinley, E. E., Stein, J. F., and Richardson, A. J., "Membrane fatty acids, reading and spelling in dyslexic and non-dyslexic adults", *European Neuropsychopharmacology* 7 (2),, 2007, pp. 116-21; and Lawrence, F., "Severely troubled boys soothed by fish oils", *Guardian*, 12 October 2006. The "John Stein" quoted in the article is one of the authors of the 2007 research. More research is underway.

3. See Henslin, E., *This is Your Brain on Joy: A Revolutionary Program for Balancing Mood, Restoring Brain Health, and Nurturing Spiritual Growth*, Nashville, Tennessee: Thomas Nelson, Inc., 2008, for dietary and supplement recommendations to calm the limbic system and

strengthen the neocortex, as well as more general information about our brains, emotions, and interpersonal relations.

4. Adapted from Francis, L., *Faith and Psychology: Personality, Religion and the Individual*, London: Darton, Longman & Todd, 2005.

5. Adapted from Kraybill, R., *Style Matters: The Kraybill Conflict Style Inventory*, Riverhouse Epress, 2005. See www.riverhouseepress.com for more information on the Kraybill Conflict Style Inventory.

6. This IC presentation of the Big 5 personality traits was created by Sara Savage.

7. See the "Couple's Dialogue Questions" developed by Harville Hendrix, *Getting the Love You Want*, London: Simon & Schuster, 1993. See also Gary Brainerd's "Conscious Dialog Process" at www. Relationship-Help.com, developed from the "Revolving Discussion Sequence" in A. Ellis and T. Crawford, *Making Intimate Connections: Seven Guidelines for Great Relationships and Better Communication*, Ballycastle, UK: Impact Publishers, 2000.

8. Adapted from *Moving Your Church Through Conflict* by Speed Leas and used by the Mennonites in their peacemaking work. For more information about Mennonite peacemaking resources, see www. bridgebuilders.co.uk.

Chapter 5

1. Baumeister, R., *Evil: Inside Human Cruelty and Violence*, New York: W. H. Freeman and Company, 1997.

2. Tetlock, P. E., "American and Soviet foreign policy rhetoric: A time series analysis", *Journal of Personality and Social Psychology*, 49, 1985, pp. 1565–85.

3. See Norcross, J. C. and Goldfried, M. R., *Handbook of Psychotherapy Integration*, Oxford: Oxford University Press, 2005; S. Palmer and R. Woolfe (Eds.), *Integrative and Eclectic Counselling and Psychotherapy*, London: SAGE Publications, 1999.

4. Relatively new, integrative therapies have been found to be more effective for people with PDs. Integrating strategies from cognitive, psychodynamic, person-centred, and systems methodologies have resulted in greater self-insight, awareness, and personal change. If you are with someone who may be struggling with a PD, there is new hope. Encourage them to seek help.

5. Bowlby, J., *A Secure Base: Clinical Applications of Attachment Theory*, Routledge: London, 1988.

6. These IC representations of PDs were created by Sara Savage.

7. Kernberg, O. E., *Borderline Conditions and Pathological Narcissism*, New York: Jason Aronson, 1975; Kohut, H., *The Analysis of the Self*, New York: International Universities Press, 1971; Kohut, H., *The Search for Self*, New York: International Universities Press, 1978.

8. Bornstein, R. F., "The Dependent Personality: Developmental, Social, and Clinical Perspectives", *Psychological Bulletin*, 112(1), 1992, pp. 3–23.

9. Kohut, H., *The Restoration of the Self*, New York: International Universities Press, 1977.

10. Chodoff, P., "The Diagnosis of Hysteria: An Overview", *American Journal of Psychiatry*, 131, 1982, pp. 1073–78.

11. Kass, F., Spitzer, R. L., and Williams, J. B. W., "An Empirical Study of the Issue of Sex Bias in the Diagnostic Criteria of DSMIII Axis II Personality Disorders", *American Psychologist*, 38, 1983, pp. 799–801.

12. Widiger, T. A., "Generalized Social Phobias Versus Avoidant Personality Disorder: A Commentary of Three Studies", *Journal of Abnormal Psychology*, 100(2), 1992, pp. 340–43.

13. Hare, R. D., Hart, S .D., and Harpur, T. J., (1991), "Psychopathy and the DSM IV Criteria for Antisocial Personality Disorder", *Journal of Abnormal Psychology*, 100, 1991, pp. 391–98.

14. Rosenhan, D. L. and Seligman, M. E. P., *Abnormal Psychology*, third edition, New York: Norton & Company, 1995.

15. Axelrod, R., *The Evolution of Cooperation*, New York: Basic Books, 1984; and also see Savage, S. and Boyd-MacMillan, E., *The Human Face of Church: A Social Psychology and Pastoral Theology Resource for Pioneer and Traditional Ministry*, London: SCM Press, 2007, chapter on "Difficult People".

16. See Norcross, J. C. and Goldfried, M. R., *Handbook of Psychotherapy Integration*, Oxford: Oxford University Press, 2005; Palmer, S. and Woolfe, R. (Eds.), *Integrative and Eclectic Counselling and Psychotherapy*, London: SAGE Publications, 1999.

17. Beck, A. T., *Cognitive Therapy for Emotional Disorders*, New York: International Universities Press, 1976.

18. Marks, I. M., *Fears and Phobias*, New York: Academic Press, 1969.

19. Kazdin, A. E. and Wilcoxon, L. A., "Systematic Desensitization and Non-specific Treatment Effects: A Methodological Evaluation", *Psychological Bulletin*, 83(5), 1976, pp. 729–58; Bandura, A., "Fearful Expectations and Avoidant Actions as Coefficients of Personal Self-efficacy", *American Psychologist*, 41(12), 1986, pp. 1239–91.

20. Kubler-Ross, E., *On Death and Dying*, New York: Macmillan, 1970;

Kubler-Ross, E., *Death, the Final Stage of Growth*, Englewood Cliffs, NJ: Prentice Hall, 1975.

Part Two
Introduction
1. Suedfeld, P., Leighton, D. C., and Conway, L. G., "Integrative Complexity and Cognitive Management in International Confrontations" in M. Fitzduff and C. E. Stout (Eds.), *The Psychology of Resolving Global Conflicts: From War to Peace*, vol.1, Nature vs. Nurture, New York: Praeger Security International, 2005, pp. 211–37.

2. See Chapter 4, Big 5 lenses, for the trait "openness to experience".

3. Thanks to Ruth Layzell for the ideas expressed here. Also see Savage, S., Watts, F., and Layzell, R., *The Beta Course*, (2003/2004), Copyright © University of Cambridge.

4. Durkheim, E., *The Clash of Civilizations and the Remaking of World Order*, New York: Simon and Schuster, 1965.

5. Boyd-MacMillan, R., *Faith that Endures: The Essential Guide to the Persecuted Church*, Grand Rapids, MI: Baker, 2006.

Chapter 6
1. Baumrind, D., "Current Patterns of Parental Authority", *Developmental Psychology*, 4 (1, pt. 2), 1971, pp. 1–103.

2. With thanks to Ofer Grosbard for his insights about Western and traditional parenting styles in O. Grosbard, *Dialogue – 123 Therapeutic Stories from Traditional Society and their Solution*, Hebrew edition: Ben-Gurion University, 2007, and O. Grosbard, *Cracking the Cultural Code*, Hebrew edition: Ben-Gurion University, 2007.

3. Baumrind, D., "Parental Disciplinary Patterns and Social Competence in Children", *Youth and Society*, 9, 1978, 238–76.

4. Maccoby, E. E. and Martin, J. A., "Socialization in the Context of the Family: Parent–child Interaction" in P. Mussen and E. M. Hetherington (Eds.), *Handbook of Child Psychology*, vol. IV: Socialization, personality, and social development, fourth edition, New York: Wiley, 1983, Chapter 1, pp. 1–101.

5. Santrock, J. W., *A Topical Approach to Life-span Development*, third edition, New York: McGraw-Hill, 2007; Rutter, M., *Helping Troubled Children*, New York: Penguin, 1975; Loeber, R., "Development and Risk Factors of Juvenile Antisocial Behaviour and Delinquency", *Clinical Psychology Review*, 10, 1990, pp. 1–41.

6. Gardner, H., *Leading Minds: An Anatomy of Leadership*, London: HarperCollins, 1996.

7. Patterson, G. R., DeBarshye, B. D., and Ramsey, E., "A developmental perspective on anti-social behaviour", *American Psychologist*, 44, 1989, pp. 329–35.

8. Savage, S., Mayo-Collins, S., and Mayo, B., *Making Sense of Generation Y: The World View of 16-25-year-olds*, London: Church House Publishing, 2006.

9. Savage, S. and Boyd-Macmillan, E., *The Human Face of Church*, London: SCM Press, 2007. See Chapter 4, "Empowering Leadership".

10. Martin, R., *The Opposable Mind: How Successful Leaders Win Through Integrative Thinking*, Boston, Massachusetts: Harvard Business Press, 2009.

Chapter 7

1. Huntingdon, S., *The Clash of Civilizations and the Remaking of World Order*, New York: Simon & Schuster, 1996.

2. Boyd-MacMillan, E. and Savage, S., *Transforming Conflict: Conflict Transformation amongst Senior Church Leaders with Different Theological Stances*, York: FCL Press, 2008.

3. Savage, S., "Towards Integrative Solutions to Moral Disputes between Conservative and Liberal Christians", *The Journal of Psychology and Christianity*, special edition, 2008.

4. Schwartz, S. H., and Boehnke, K., "Evaluating the Structure of Human Values with Confirmatory Factor Analysis", *Journal of Research in Personality*, 38(3), 2004, 230; Schwartz, S. H. and Huismans, S. "Value Priorities and Religiosity in Four Western Religions", *Social Psychology Quarterly*, 58 (2), 1995, pp. 88–107.

5. Liht, J. and Savage, S., "Being Muslim, Being British: An Intervention to Prevent Violent Radicalisation by Fostering Self-integration through Value Complexity", unpublished manuscript, University of Cambridge, 2009.

6. Liht, J. and Savage, S., "Identifying Young Muslims Susceptible to Violent Radicalisation: Psychological theory and recommendations" in M. Sharpe (Ed.), *Suicide Bombing: Psychological and Other Imperatives*, IOS Publishers, NATO publication, 2008.

7. Hunsberger, B., Alisat, S., Pancer, M., and Pratt, M., "Religious Fundamentalism and Religious Doubts: Content, Connections and Complexity of Thinking", *The International Journal for the Psychology of Religion*, 6 (3), 1996, pp. 201–20.

8. Savage, S., "Towards Integrative Solutions to Moral Disputes between Conservative and Liberal Christians", *The Journal of Psychology and Christianity*, special edition, 2008.

9. Sandoval, C., *Theory Out of Bounds: Methodology of the Oppressed*, University of Minneapolis Press, 2000.

10. Satterfield, J. M. and Seligman, M. E. P., "Military Aggression and Risk Predicted by Explanatory Style", *Psychological Science*, 5 (2), 1994, pp. 77–82.

Chapter 8

1. The information in this paragraph was part of a speech delivered by Michael Stopford, NATO Deputy Assistant Secretary General, Strategic Communications, Public Diplomacy Department, at a NATO/ ESF/ISAF conference on Radicalization held in Brussels, Belgium, 20–22 April 2009.

2. Hendrix, H., *Getting the Love You Want*, London: Simon & Schuster, 1993.

3. See Gerhardt, S., *Why Love Matters: How Affection Shapes a Baby's Brain*, London: Routledge, 2004.

4. See Gerhardt, S., *Why Love Matters: How Affection Shapes a Baby's Brain*, London: Routledge, 2004.

5. See Reich, K. H., *Developing the Horizons of the Mind: Relational and Contextual Reasoning and the Resolution of Cognitive Conflict*, Cambridge, UK: Cambridge University Press, 2002.

Index